e-Business

e-Business

*How to make money running a
business on the internet*

BRUCE DURIE

How To Books

Published by How To Books Ltd,
3 Newtec Place, Magdalen Road,
Oxford OX4 1RE, United Kingdom.
Tel: (01865) 793806. Fax: (01865) 248780.
email: info@howtobooks.co.uk
http://www.howtobooks.co.uk

British Library Cataloguing in Publication Data.
A catalogue record for this book is available from
the British Library.

Edited by Diana Brueton
Cover design by Shireen Nathoo Design
Cover image by PhotoDisc
Cover copy by Sallyann Sheridan

Produced for How To Books by Deer Park Productions.
Typeset by Anneset, Weston-super-Mare, N Somerset.
Printed and bound by Cromwell Press, Trowbridge, Wiltshire.

NOTE: The material contained in this book is set out in good
faith for general guidance and no liability can be accepted
for loss or expense incurred as a result of relying in particular
circumstances on statements made in the book. Laws and
regulations are complex and liable to change, and readers should
check the current position with the relevant authorities before
making personal arrangements.

Contents

List of Illustrations

Preface

WHAT IS e-BUSINESS? A THOUGHT FOR SENIOR MANAGERS

I was recently at a conference on the subject of **electronic commerce** and the **digital revolution** in business, with an audience mostly of senior managers and owners of small and medium-sized enterprises (SMEs). They were treated to a series of talks from the great and the good of the business world, the telecomms companies, government and computer manufacturers. Their talks had titles like 'Do e-business or die' and 'e-volution is revolution' and 'e is for everything'. Rather than looking enlightened as the day progressed, most of the audience became more and more glum and bewildered. I suggested at one point that a suitable title for the conference would have been 'e = MD(scared)' and got a rousing cheer from all the business people there.

A number of things were clear:

- Everyone accepted that there was a growing place for more and better electronic business-to-business communication.

- They all knew that if they didn't do it, their competitors would, and then where would they be?

- They had mostly taken advantage of the widely available help, advice, guidance, free (or subsidised) consultancy and local seminars organised by various arms of government, and they still didn't have a clue what to do next.

- They were getting almost daily calls from computer hardware manufacturers, software producers, web designers, internet market specialists, change management consultants and economic development officials, all claiming to have a large part of (in some cases *all*) the solution. And yet they were still bewildered.

- Their internal IT departments saw e-business as an opportunity to hire more and more staff to support yet more computers and new software in an increasingly complex network.

- The company board members mostly wanted to go and hide under a nice, warm duvet until it all went away.

  Except it isn't going to go away. **Electronic business** (explained in a lot more detail later) is here to stay and – surprise, surprise – *most companies are already doing it.*
  This book starts from these perspectives:

- Companies want to conduct more business using electronic, computer-based and telecomms-enabled processes.

- The apparently large number of decisions to be made is not as complex as it looks.

- The whole exercise can be approached like any other business change.

- It's a lot easier than everyone will try to persuade you.

- It needn't cost much, except time and thought.

  It will show you:

- What e-business consists of.

- How to use existing tools and processes to re-engineer your business into an e-business.

- How to determine your own e-business strategy.

- How to set up e-mail campaigns, electronic storefronts and transactions processes.

- How to make sure you are legally and financially secure.

- How to expand your market from local to global.

It need not cost you a fortune
If you are a global multinational with a thousand products, sales outlets in a hundred countries and a turnover in the billions, you probably already have a sophisticated and expensive e-business operation. In fact, if you don't, you won't be a global multinational etc etc much longer. But the same principles and practices are available to the smallest of companies and at marginal cost. The savings and increased sales will more than repay the effort. *If done properly.*

Make a fortune on the internet

Yes, there is a sure-fire way to make a fortune on the internet. Simply take out an advert (or set up a web page) that says 'Make a fortune on the internet' and charge the gullible a reasonable sum to receive their starter pack. This consists of instructions to take out an advert (or set up a web page) that says 'Make a fortune on the internet' and charge the gullible a reasonable sum to receive their starter pack. And so on.

A variation on this is an update of the old and now discredited pyramid selling techniques, where someone will pay you money if you refer to them people who will recruit others to pay money if referred and if they recruit people who . . . it's a chain letter, in other words. Yes, if you persuade ten people to pay you £100 you have £1,000 and if each of them persuades ten people to pay £100 of which £10 come to you, you have another £1,000 and so it goes on. But it doesn't take much thought or mathematical ability to see that seven steps in this process would involve ten million people (just about every wage-earner in the UK) and you would have earned £7,000, and what are the chances of that happening? Especially since everyone else would expect to earn the same? And you could end up getting ten million e-mails offering you the same opportunity.

But if you really want to start a genuine business on the internet, or use internet techniques to improve your existing business, and if you are prepared to take the advice seriously, then start reading. Along the way there will be case studies and horror stories to encourage and dismay you. And, with luck, to teach you a few lessons.

Should you feel threatened by e-business? Yes.

There was a time, only a few years ago, when to challenge an existing business took immense resources, capital and courage. Now even the largest, well-established businesses are feeling the heat of e-business. Consider:

• What would it take to set up a car dealership in your town alongside the existing half-dozen or more with the track records, buildings, stock of expensive vehicles and customer base? But now various internet entrepreneurs – '**Netrepreneurs**' is the buzz word – will offer you a great deal on a car direct from the manufacturer if you join a purchasing cartel. Or they will find the car you want in Europe and ship it home – and they never even have to actually see the car in question. Meanwhile, you get a bargain.

• If you can choose and book a holiday on-line and arrange flights, hotel, car hire, tickets to local attractions and insurance with your PC, why go to a high street travel agent?

• Want a new computer? Trudge down to your local store and choose from the limited range on offer. Or pick any model offered by Dell, Gateway, IBM, Time or a plethora of other manufacturers and have it delivered to your door.

• Fed up standing in queues at the bank? Move your accounts and standing orders to FirstDirect, Egg or another on-line bank and stay at home while you organise your finances.

• Like the latest Bowie album? Not sure? Download a segment and if you like it, download the entire thing, play it as MP3 in the background while you work, transfer it to your portable MP3 player for the car or the train and write it to a CD for listening to in the other room. Or go and try to get sense out of the spotty youth who works in the local record store on Saturdays.

• Want to learn French, brush up your computer skills, master trigonometry or take a management diploma? Don't fancy taking a day off work every week to attend the college or university or turning up every Wednesday evening for a year? Do it at home by a combination of on-line and distance learning.

• Run out of milk? No, you haven't, because your intelligent fridge has spotted the fact, along with the imminent danger of going bread-deprived and the van will be round in half-an-hour.

OK, the last one is still in the hype stage, but all the rest are solid, practical realities. No wonder large companies are either reformulating themselves into internet-only businesses – like Dell – or have set up internet-only subsidiaries – like Dixons with Freeserve or Egg (which is Prudential, although they don't even say so in the adverts).

Should you feel threatened by e-business? No.
Everything someone else has done, you can do too. The internet brings global sales opportunities to your back bedroom, portakabin hut, industrial unit on the local business part, multinational headquarters and corner shop.

There are two opposing trends operating here, and they are not at odds with each other. As the world of business becomes more global, with large companies merging to become larger companies, they are all struggling to dominate the internet. Yet at the same time the fact of the internet has democratised business to the extent that it is easier than ever for an individual or small group of people to start, manage and grow a successful operation. The internet can turn us all into netrepreneurs – and all we need is courage, imagination and (possibly) this book!

Bruce Durie

PART 1

The Ten Steps to e-Business

Introduction

e-BUSINESS IS NOT JUST e-COMMERCE

Let's agree to define e-commerce as an electronic way of processing financial transactions, either between businesses and the public (customers) or business to business. This has been happening for a number of years, mostly in the following guises:

- **Transferring assets** electronically between large financial institutions (eg share transactions).
- **Electronic data interchange** (**EDI**) – for example, scanning items in a retail store and using the information for stock control, marketing information etc.
- **Banking** – banks move billions of pounds every day amongst each other when you cash, deposit or send a cheque.
- **Automated teller machines** (**ATM**) – the 'hole-in-the-wall' cash dispenser.
- **Home and office banking** (**HOBS**) – pioneered and popularised by the Bank of Scotland, HOBS allows immediate control of bank accounts using a dedicated terminal linked to a phone line.

All of this is extremely useful and widely implemented, but it has three main drawbacks for adoption by most businesses:

- it is extremely expensive
- it usually requires dedicated lines, networks and equipment
- it is available only to large organisations, for reasons of cost and operating complexity.

But a few years ago a new development put this technology within everyone's grasp – the internet.

THE INTERNET AND THE WEB

This is not the place to retread definitions of internet (the net) and world wide web (the web) in any great detail, except to lay out the definitions which are the most commonly accepted and which will be used in this book.

The internet is essentially an agreement between computers to share information and the hardware, telecomms infrastructure (phone lines, cables and exchanges) and protocols to make that happen. There are some 25 million servers providing information and services and holding text, graphics, programs, video and sound. Some are merely gateways which route traffic and some are the hosts for content placed there, owned and administered by others. They communicate through the **internet backbone**.

The web is a graphical component of the internet, allowing control over fonts and other display content by **hypertext markup language (HTML)** and the use of **hyperlinks** (clicking on a word, image or picture in a web page links you to another page in the same or a different web site). The web lets you download programs, text, video, audio, graphics etc onto your computer from a server, either via your browser or by a special protocol called **FTP** which requires its own software.

Other components of the internet are **e-mail** (electronic mail), **newsgroups** and **bulletin boards** (which allow people of like mind to share information via a network of linked newsgroups called the **usenet**) and **internet relay chat** (**IRC**), which uses specialised software for synchronous (at the same time) communication between users, whether by keyboard or voice.

The internet grew out of **Arpanet**, a computer network designed to safeguard military communications from attack. Then it became the routine communication tool of the academic community. The addition of the web, and the wide availability of browser programs (such as Netscape and Internet Explorer) and e-mail clients (eg Eudora, Pegasus or Outlook Express) has made the internet accessible to everyone. Its great advantages are:

- It uses the sort of computer hardware which is within the grasp of almost any family, school, business or group.
- It uses the standard and wide-spread telephone system.
- There is a vast and growing range of software to allow almost anyone to do almost anything they want.

The internet means that any business can become an e-business. And e-business is not just e-commerce.

e-BUSINESS – WHAT IT MEANS FOR YOU

For most businesses, e-business means the combination of three sets of activities.

1 Internal business processes – all the existing components of your business, which can be handled better, faster or cheaper with technology and which can be integrated with the other two.
2 Customer and supplier relationships – your advertising, marketing, customer support, customer contact, order processing and delivery scheduling can be managed with the right software, hardware and organisation.
3 Transactions – this is what most people mean by e-commerce: the movement of money down wires using 100 per cent recyclable electrons.

Apart from adopting the sort of e-commerce practices that have until now been the province of major companies, the widespread adoption of the internet and the web means that all businesses can now do these things and more:

• Operate globally – you are not restricted to the customers who walk past your shop window, see your listing in trade directories or the local paper or get your leaflets through their doors.
• Expand the customer base – any other business or private individual with access to the internet is a potential customer.
• Compete effectively – rest assured all your existing competitors and even more new ones you never knew you had are taking this very seriously indeed.
• Process orders, payments and deliveries automatically – all the normal business processes concerned with securing and fulfilling orders can be streamlined.
• Advertise widely – global brand development is now possible.
• Focus the marketing effort – building up profiles of your current and potential customers on-line will allow more targeted approaches.
• Cut costs – by streamlining your administrative processes and making the best use of stock handling routines, you can save money.
• Integrate your business activities – pull together all the things you use computers for at present.

YOU'RE ALREADY DOING IT

The chances are you are using a number of e-business tools at present. Anyone who confirms an order by phone or fax is doing e-business. Anyone who sends a customer an e-mail is doing e-business. Any company which keeps its accounts, client contact details, supplier database and stock records on a computer is doing e-business. Any company with a web site is doing e-business. Any business which regularly checks out the competition's web site, or uses the web to research markets, is doing e-business. The three questions to ask yourself are:

1 How well are you doing this?
2 How integrated are these different components of e-business?
3 What else could you do, or do better, electronically?

THE TEN STEPS OF e-BUSINESS

This book will take you through the processes involved in e-business by a series of ten steps. These are:

* Step 1 Get started – assemble what you need
* Step 2 Get a good idea – decide what you are selling, whether it is products or services or both
* Step 3 Get e-mail – organise your existing e-mail accounts (or establish new ones) for marketing and selling
* Step 4 Get a web site – set up your own web site or make use of an existing one
* Step 5 Get a domain name – establish your brand identity on the web
* Step 6 Get visitors – attract people to your web site and drive traffic
* Step 7 Know your visitors – track and measure your success
* Step 8 Improve your site – supercharge your web site with e-commerce and other performance enhancements
* Step 9 Find new customers – discover and target potential customers
* Step 10 Start selling online – secure transactions and merchant services.

TIPS AND TRICKS FOR e-BUSINESS

The second part of the book will provide checklists, ideas, hints and tips and cautionary tales to help you take your e-business further.

At the end of the book are resource lists – where to get tools, which web sites to look at, which newsletters to subscribe to and other useful information.

If you get lost in the jargon, there is a glossary.

Step 1

Get Started: Assemble What You Need

ORGANISE YOUR TIME

It is perfectly possible to fit your e-business creation into your spare time. It does not need long, dedicated periods of concentrated work. In fact, most of the slog is just thinking.

Your first step, as with starting any business, should be writing a **business plan**. If you have never done this before there are many business aids on-line, free to download, which can help you. Don't follow them slavishly, but get a feel for the areas they cover. One example is Planit but there are many others – search for 'business plan software' in any search engine. One way to think about this is, if you were presenting your idea to a bank manager:

- How would you explain it simply in a few sentences?
- What questions would you be asked?
- What is it going to cost?
- What will the revenue be?
- What are the opportunities and can you quantify them?
- What is the competition?
- How will you promote your e-business?

Brunel University has a good set of links to business startup resources (*http://sol.brunel.ac.uk/~jarvis/bola/businesses/busplan/web.html*)   as does the American Small Business Administration (*http://www.sbaonline.sba.gov/starting/businessplan.html*).

ORGANISE YOUR MOTIVATION

Do you have what it takes? What do you need to be successful? This quiz may help you find out your strong business skills and where you may need to improve them. Answer each question with a 1–3 score (1 = no; 2 = sometimes; 3 = definitely).

1 Are you a leader in group settings or activities?   ❏

2 Can you finish a project, even if it means late nights and low recognition from others? ❑

3 Do you have many hobbies (besides TV and video/computer games)? ❑

4 Do you like meeting new people? ❑

5 Do you like to set goals and achieve them? ❑

6 Do you like working alone? ❑

7 Do you manage your time? ❑

8 Do you often think of new ways to do things? ❑

9 Have you had a past success in planning and carrying through a project to completion? ❑

10 When something goes wrong, do you learn from it? ❑

11 Will you take a calculated risk to achieve a goal? ❑

12 Would others consider you a positive sort of person? ❑

Total: ❑

Quiz scoring

- If most of your scores are 3s and your total is 30 or over, you have a strong entrepreneurial bent.

- If most of your scores are 2s with some 3s and your total is 22 or over you probably have what it takes to be self-employed.

- If you scored mostly 1s and 2s, with a total under 16, consider whether you have the attitude and commitment to starting your own business.

- If you didn't understand what was meant by most of the questions, there are lots of nice, safe jobs in the Civil Service or selling burgers.

Now give the test to someone you know and love (and who will be honest) and get them to complete it with you in mind. Have a bunch of flowers handy in case you fall out.

ORGANISE YOUR MIND

You will have your own set of reasons why you want to, and another of reasons why you can't, won't or don't know where or how to start. There is probably a long line of people at your door with similar lists of pros and cons.

If you are running an existing business with a board or a group of partners, they will want to know that you have thought through the whys and wherefores and have considered the alternatives to not going down the e-business route and the pitfalls in the way. Arguments for and against follow.

REASONS TO DO e-BUSINESS

- A business can expand its operations from local or regional to national and global at much lower cost than by conventional means.

- How difficult (and how expensive) is it at present to update your product list, catalogue, price list, contact details and brochures?

- How many ways do you collect payments now – cheques, cash, bank drafts, credit cards, foreign currency transactions etc? These can be integrated.

- How much paper do you lose track of every day, week, month, year?

- If your customers find it easier to deal with someone else on-line, how long will they remain your customers?

- Information collection is easier – if the customer fills in a web form this is less labour-intensive than someone copying down details over the phone then transcribing them to a computer (assuming that happens at all!).

- It is easier to contact your customer base – one e-mail can be sent to a large number of people.

- Many of the companies you do business with at present – and a lot of those you might hope to do business with in the future – are going down the e-business route. You may find yourself cut off from clients or suppliers if you do not adopt similar practices.

- You can integrate a number of disparate arms of the business – is your client payment database the same as your customer contact database? If not, why not?

- You can provide additional services not possible at present – on-line progress checking of dispatched orders or payments is only one example.

PROBLEMS WITH e-BUSINESS

- Can you keep your promises? If you sell something to Australia or Mongolia, are you confident you can get it there, on schedule and in one piece?

- If you trade in different countries, there is the complication of multiple currency transactions (but this can be addressed).

- Is what you are selling, advertising or providing and the way you provide it legal in every country?

- Does it fit with your existing business model? (If not, change your existing business model – or develop a new one and run both in parallel.)

- Is it just for IT-based companies selling information or digital products and no good for tangible things? (Oh no it isn't – you can buy a book, a car or a pair of trousers.)

- Are all of your customers or suppliers on-line? (Probably not. But consider – do you want them as customers or suppliers if they cost more to maintain?)

- Does everyone speak English? No, so a multi-language facility may be necessary. (But in how many languages do you print your current information? Probably only one.)

- There are millions and millions of business web sites, on-line stores and internet adverts out there – so how will yours stand out? (But how well does your business stand out at the moment?)

- Are you organised to take advantage of internet opportunities? (So get organised.)

- You may encounter cultural differences – does your clever advertising slogan mean something totally different to a Korean?

- Do you feel you have nothing to gain? (Ah. Read on!)

WHAT'S TO GAIN?

If you can answer Yes to any one of the questions in List A below and Yes to any one of the questions in List B, e-business can bring you advantages:

List A
- Would you like to make and receive payments   ❏
  electronically?
- Would you like to expand into new markets?   ❏
- Does your advertising and promotions budget not stretch   ❏
  as far as you would like and is it constraining your
  expansion into new markets?
- Do you have a 'static' web site (no e-commerce or limited   ❏
  interactivity)?

List B
- Does your business sell easily-shipped products?   ❏
- Do you produce a printed catalogue or product list?   ❏
- Do you sell information?   ❏
- Do you sell something specialised (product or service)?   ❏
- Do you offer customer support by telephone?   ❏

ORGANISE YOUR BUSINESS

You may have one or more existing business tools which you would like to build into your e-business. These might include:

- a mail-order catalogue
- product brochures

- data sheets
- drawings and diagrams
- information packs
- news releases
- newsletters
- a discussion forum
- an existing web site.

If you don't have e-mail, consult Step 3. (page 43)
If you don't have a web site, consult Step 4. (page 65)

ORGANISE YOUR COMPUTER

In order to do e-business you will need the following equipment and software:

- A **computer**, capable of connecting to the internet and powerful enough to run the programs you will need. By preference it should be a PC (or an iMac) running Windows 98.

- **Dial-up software**.

- An **e-mail program**.

- A **web browser**.

- A **news reader program**.

- An **FTP client**.

- A connection to and an account with an **internet service provider (ISP)**.

All these will now be examined in more detail.

Hardware
If you have a computer it should ideally be a Pentium II or III (or equivalent AMD processor) PC with at least a 250MHz **CPU**, a 200MB hard disc, 64K of **RAM**, a **CD-Rom**, a **modem** (see below), a decent graphics card and full duplex sound card, a colour monitor (preferably 17-inch or larger to save eye strain) capable of displaying 800×600 resolution, keyboard and mouse. The type of PC sold in high street or mail order outlets for under £1,000 should suffice.

Make sure it has (or upgrade to) Windows 98 as your operating system.

This is not to say that a decent e-business can't be run on an old 486 with a 15-inch black-and-white monitor under Windows 3.1. But some of your options will be limited and you won't get the full benefit of many of the new 32-bit programs available and you won't see your own and other web pages in full glorious colour. Most modern internet and web software is designed to run under Windows 95 and/or 98, so it is best to install or upgrade to these.

However, you do not need to rush out and buy the latest all-singing, all-dancing multimedia monster with a go-faster stripe and enough oomph to run a space mission – unless you really want to and it will be useful. If, for instance, you are considering a new PC for home to use for education, multimedia games etc, choose a machine that will suit all likely purposes.

There will come a time when you want a separate machine for your business, but you'll have made so much money from your e-business by then you'll be able to lease an IBM mainframe and manage your global company with a massive Oracle installation. But if you're that rich, why are you still working?

Note: This book makes no further reference to Macs

A statement like the one in this heading unleashes a stream of furious e-mails, letters, phone calls and confrontations at meetings about why Macs are so good, why Microsoft might not be, and why am I so prejudiced that I am part of the conspiracy? This is essentially a religious war and one I have no interest in joining – the fact is, there are many more PCs running Microsoft Windows than there are Macs and a lot more software for windows and PCs. It is not me you have to convince but the one billion PC/Windows owners out there. If IBM couldn't dislodge Windows with its own OS2 operating system and Lotus can't make everyone change from Microsoft Office to SmartSuite, what chance have the rest of us? End of discussion.

Modem

56K
If your PC came with a 56K Flex modem, fine. If you have to buy one separately, get an external modem. This will make it easier to change if and when you decide to install **ISDN** (see below). Get a fax/voice/data modem so that you can send faxes as well as internet data – most modern modems have this facility as standard and include

fax sending/receiving software as well. Bear in mind that a fax will usually be sent (and stored when you receive one) as bitmap images – a graphic – so it will usually not be possible to edit the text.

Modems use the standard telephone line and communicate by making noises down it which computers can translate back and forth as information. The '56k' refers to the maximum speed (57,600 bits per second or 56Kbps) your modem can transfer data. In practice speeds are much slower than that – they are determined by the amount of traffic on the network and the speed of the port on your computer the modem is connected to. It is rarely faster than 4KB (4,000 Bytes, not bits) per second, so a 1MB file will take about 4–10 minutes to download (1MB = 1,000,000 Bytes ÷ 4,000 Bps = 250 seconds = about 4 minutes, but you won't get that speed all the time). A 4KB image will take 1–2 seconds to load in a web site.

To minimise cost and time spent waiting, do your downloads and uploads when no one else is. Calls are cheaper after 6pm or 8pm and at weekends. America wakes up in what is the early afternoon for us, and instantly hits the e-mail, so things are very slow until at least 10pm. Other bottlenecks occur at 6–8pm (home e-mail and homework time), 7–8am ('I'll just upload these files before I go to the office'), early Saturday evening ('Check and see if we won the lottery') and late Saturday evening ('Hello dear, I've just brought the guys back to show them that football site I found last week').

ISDN
This uses the same copper wire but is cleverer at transferring the data, so it is about twice as fast. Usually two digital lines are available so it can be four times as fast if you use both at once (but you pay for two phone calls). ISDN is a time-saver and a potential money-saver if you plan to do lots of large uploads and downloads, but it is more expensive. This will change with the appearance of **cable modems** and **ADSL**. Cable modems will be available from whoever supplies your phone lines and/or TV by cable. ADSL is an even cleverer technology which takes ISDN a stage further and may be even cheaper – no more per minute than a standard phone call. Ask your current phone line provider what plans there are for ISDN, cable modems and/or ADSL.

If you do decide to use ISDN, make sure your ISP supports it, or change to one which can. **OSP**s (see below) tend not to, but this is changing.

BT offers (at the time of writing) a halfway house to ISDN called Home Highway. It converts an existing standard phone line into two digital lines. There is an installation charge and the rental and call charges are higher. However, rates change all the time, so check the latest situation.

There are also deals for people who change to or from cable providers or BT. There are also loyalty deals for *not* changing. It is worth enquiring.

Leased lines
An established business may choose to install a **leased line**, your very own phone cable. This is no faster than ISDN but does have the advantage of being a permanent connection between you and an ISP, is 'open' all the time and has no call charges. However, it will cost several thousands of pounds per year (more if you are far from a major town) and also needs specialised router equipment. This is only really an economic option if, for instance, you plan to operate your own server and need a permanent connection, or if there is to be a great deal of large data transfer – an architectural or design practice, say, using the internet to send and receive large CAD files or drawings.

The next step up is a high-speed 2Mb leased line (about 15–30 times as fast as ISDN) but it is a specialised option only really suitable for and affordable by major companies, large ISPs and villains in James Bond movies with a thirst for world domination. Still, it's amazing how many company chairmen fall into the latter category, so do ask.

Which?
All in all 56K is fine for those starting out, with ISDN as an option (especially for established businesses) and ADSL will suit most people when it arrives.

Dial-up software
If you have Windows 95 or 98, you will already have a piece of mysterious software called **TCP/IP** or **socket manager** and you will probably remain blithely unaware of its existence as it does its job quietly in the background. If not, you will have to acquire it. Most ISPs (see below) provide it as part of the sign-up package.

You will also need **dial up networking** (in your My Computer desktop icon) which controls the numbers your PC dials and how. When you choose an ISP the configuring software may come ready to do the hard work for you. Alternatively, there is an **internet connection wizard**.

An e-mail program

If you have or install Microsoft Internet Explorer 4 or 5, you will have an e-mail client called Outlook Express. This is ideal for most e-business purposes and more specialised functions can be handled by other programs dealt with in Step 3 (page 43). Netscape Communicator users will have Netscape Mail which is also a fine e-mail client.

Other popular e-mail clients such as Pegasus or Eudora operate much the same way. The commercial versions (the ones you pay for, not the disabled form that came free with something) will have more features and options.

One thing to watch is the protocol your e-mail client uses. There are two common mail protocols, **SMTP** (**Simple Mail Transfer Protocol**) and **POP3** (**Post Office Protocol 3**). Many ISPs use both – SMTP for receiving and POP3 for sending – so your chosen e-mail client should be able to handle both. Some ISPs (Demon is an example) use only SMTP, so you will need an e-mail program capable of supporting SMTP to both receive and send.

Usually, your ISP will have a mail server called something like *mail.isp.co.uk*.

A web browser

Microsoft has made Internet Explorer hard to avoid and it is used as the main browser by over half of PC owners. Netscape, previously the market leader (if giving software away free can be called a 'market'), has most of the rest. It makes sense to have both installed – you may want to test out your web site for compatibility with both browsers and each of them has advantages and tricks the other can't do. Resist the temptation to choose another browser like Opera – excellent though many of them are, you are trying to establish a service that is compatible with the rest of humanity, not prove your independence of spirit.

If you sign up with an ISP, the chances are you will be offered IE5 (and Outlook Express) or possibly Netscape on the CD or as part of the download. There is no harm in overwriting your existing installations with these as you can change the options (and remove the irritating logos) later.

If not, they are widely available free on the front of PC magazines or by downloading from Microsoft and Netscape respectively (see Appendix).

Get the latest versions of the browser of your choice. IE5 comes with Outlook Express as its mail and news reader, and FrontPage

Express, a web design program. Netscape Communicator 4.6 or higher should come with Navigator (the browser), Messenger (the mail and news reader), Composer (a simple web page editor/designer) and an Address Book.

Plug-ins and ActiveX Controls

The standard IE or Netscape browser cannot necessarily handle all the file types it will encounter – audio, video, 3-d rendering etc – but these can be managed by installing additional, specialised programs. Netscape uses Plug-ins, IE uses ActiveX and these are converging so that soon both will handle either. Generally, if your browser detects a file of unknown type, it will direct you to a Plug-in page where you can download and install the correct software. A lot of options come pre-installed.

A news reader program

There are over 40,000 newsgroups out there, some of which will be a useful source of information for your business and a valuable advertising mechanism. News readers are included with Internet Explorer 4 or 5 (as part of Outlook Express, but Internet News is also available free) and built into Netscape Communicator. Typically, your ISP will have a news server called *news.isp.co.uk* or something similar, but check for the correct name.

An FTP client

File transfer protocol (FTP) is the commonest way to download and upload web files. Both IE5 and Netscape come with a Publisher function on board (essentially a dedicated FTP client) but you may wish to get a more flexible program for uploading, such as FTP Voyager, WS-FTP or CuteFTP. Often, a web site – especially one which features a lot of downloads, such as a software site or a graphics site – will have a dedicated ftp server, usually called *ftp.isp.co.uk* as distinct from *www.isp.co.uk,* its main web site.

ISPs, OSPs and WSPs

An ISP (internet service provider) is essentially a link to the internet which you can use as your gateway. At the very least they provide a dial-up number to access their system. Many also offer software set-up programs (on CD, by download or sometimes on-line) and e-mail access. Some provide free or cheap web space and a domain name that is usually a variant of their own – your e-mail can be *i.smith@thisisp.co.uk* and your web domain *www.mydomain.thisisp.co.uk.* There may be no content whatsoever associated with an ISP, beyond its own home page, possibly an on-line help facility and some basic contact information.

There has been a recent trend towards **free ISPs** of late – all you pay are the phone calls – but most of them require that you install a customised browser bearing their logos, enter via a home page loaded with adverts and retail opportunities, have all your **cookies options** enabled (so they can hoover your PC for information about you) and often require that you have **caller line ID forwarding** enabled so they know who you are and where you live. In many cases these are companies which were not previously in the internet business, such as Tesco, Virgin, Boots, WH Smith etc – in other words, *they have become e-businesses.* And if they can do it, why shouldn't you?

There are also **full-service ISPs** whose business is providing commercial web space, e-mail and other services for those who wish to operate real web sites.

An **OSP (online service provider)** is more than just an ISP – it has a vast range of its own content such as information pages, databases and services. Good (or rather, well-known) examples are Compuserve and AOL. Actually, they're the same outfit although promoted separately. They are about to become part of a larger Time-Warner-EMI media conglomerate which will doubtless merge with other companies providing telecomms, mobile phones, movies, TV, groceries, books etc and will have its own seat at the United Nations.

The aspiration of every OSP is to keep you so entranced by the wealth of provision that you never have to go to the rest of the internet to read the news, check the weather, buy a car, book a holiday, look up the spelling of 'minuscule', access a **forum** (a bulletin board with a particular subject matter), get software or chat to other subscribers. They tend to charge a monthly rate (on top of phone calls) but this is being threatened by the emergence of free ISPs, many of which are fast becoming OSPs – they offer lots of content and dedicated services.

Often the content is provided by a third party who pays for the privilege of being there in front of so many million customers, and in some cases you pay an additional fee for accessing the service in questions – to check a credit rating, get a share price, search a database and the like.

A **WSP (web service provider)** provides only hosting on servers – it's where your web site physically resides. Your WSP could be your ISP, but doesn't have to be. You could use an ISP for dial-up and host your site(s) on the server(s) of one or more WSPs. Alternatively, they could be one and the same.

Which?

OSPs generally do not support ISDN or other high-speed links – if you're paying by the minute it's not really in their interest for you to zoom in and log out again quickly. Web space made available to you is part of their larger site. You may only be able to e-mail others registered with that OSP. On the other hand, the forums tend to be excellent (software support, for instance) and have lots of downloads. They are likely to have a local access number wherever you are, so you can check your e-mail in Cibu without making an expensive long-distance call. And they charge for anything they can – costs may spiral for the unwary surfer. They do tend to be easy to use (even for children or beginners) with simple installation routines and you can usually trust the content.

Free ISPs have the great advantage of being free (except for the phone call) but tend to have rather primitive web space (no database integration, no scripts and no e-commerce), provide e-mail and domains which are subsets of their own, operate only in one country via a 'local' (0845) number and hound you with what they want to sell. But they're free – did I say that already? They usually come with idiot-proof installation software. However, they do tend to like you to have cookies enabled and to permit **caller line identification** (**CLID**, see below).

ISPs which are not free offer, for a fixed monthly, quarterly or annual fee, full-function web space (the ability to run programs and databases, albeit at an additional cost), access to CGI scripts and other web goodies, fast lines, custom web design and e-commerce facilities (at extra cost). In other words, they are usually WSPs as well. They don't usually hassle you with must-buy offers or take advertising revenue from third parties who pester you. They may not, however, offer proper e-mail, but will do **e-mail forwarding** (see Step 3, page 57). They will also (at a further cost) establish your domain name for you and register it.

WSPs may only offer the web services outlined above, and not dial-up or e-mail. You will need an ISP as well.

Just to make this clearer – my main dial-up (my ISP) is ConnectFree. They also support my e-mail. I do have some sites hosted with them, so they are my WSP as well, for those sites. Because ConnectFree does not offer some of the trickier aspects of web programming (CGI access, FrontPage extensions, database support), sites which require these services are hosted with another WSP, FirstNet, who would dearly love to be my one-and-only ISP as well. I have just decided to sign up with Telewest, who are providing an unbeatable deal on dial-up charges called Surf Unlimited (albeit with technical hitches), so I may move to them as my main ISP in due course. This won't stop me taking e-mail and web space services from the other two.

Choose

A large, established business is probably best going for an account with a full-service ISP/WSP, after establishing its own domain name. If e-mail is not provided, ask about e-mail forwarding. You will still need e-mail, however, so an account with one of the large OSPs may be necessary as well. If each member of your staff has one, they can access e-mails when abroad. The OSP may have useful online data-bases – company register searches, shares information, business news-groups and the like.

A new e-business is going to need:

1 A 'real' domain name (not *jim.thisfreeone.co.uk*)
2 'Real' e-mail (not *jim@jim.thisfreeone.co.uk*)
3 'Real' web space (where e-commerce can be run).

This is all available free or very cheap.

SUBVERT YOUR FREE ISP

So you picked up a free internet CD with your groceries and you have installed it. Your e-mail address is *marymack@freethingy.com* and you have 10MB of web space waiting at *http://www.marymack.freethingy.com*. But four things bother you:

1 You are fed up with the 'Supplied by FreeThingy' banner and logo on the Internet Explorer they kindly provided. Go to the Program Files/Internet Explorer folder and delete a sub-folder called Signup. If you are nervous about deleting it, rename it ($ignup for example).

2 You hate the first web page they send you to and you never want to see another offer for cheap broccoli or holidays in Bournemouth. But you are not stuck with it. Find one you prefer – a search engine like AltaVista (*http://www.altavista.co.uk*) for

instance – and make it your start page. Make sure the chosen web page is open in your browser before you do the following:

- Netscape 4: Click Edit, Preferences, Navigator, Navigator starts with Home Page, Use Current Page
- Internet Explorer 4: Click View, Internet Options, General, Home Page, Use Current
- Internet Explorer 5: Click Tools, Internet Options, General, Home Page, Use Current

You can still use their free dial-up number even if you never go to their site again.

3   They won't allow e-commerce sites on their free web space and it wouldn't work anyway. So, once you have established your own domain and web space elsewhere, have a single page on the FreeThingy site that contains nothing but a link saying 'This site has moved to *http://www.marymack.co.uk*' just in case anyone finds it and wonders where you are.

4   Lots of people know your *marymack@freethingy.com* e-mail address and you don't want to lose it. Simple – you can run more than one e-mail account on your e-mail client, and you can also have all other e-mail you set up later (*mary@marymack.co.uk*) forwarded to the original one. See page 57 for details.

FREE DIAL-UP, DOMAINS, WEB SPACE, E-MAIL ETC

At least one free ISP offers all of the above, including the ability to run e-business software. This will certainly do until you need to move up to a large, full-service ISP, and even then you will find it useful.

The provider in question is ConnectFree and it offers two types of service.

1   The first is at *http://www.connectfree.co.uk* (click on Free Internet). This can provide you with a dial-up number (including ISDN), a domain (of the form *http://www.mydomain.connectfree.co.uk*), web space and e-mail (of the *helen@mydomain.connectfree.co.uk* type). This is fine for many purposes and may be a useful 'first' account, for home and personal use, say. Follow the procedures and **print out** all pages with information on (such as host names, passwords etc) as you will forget them later.

2   The second is at *http://www.connectfree.co.uk* (click on Free
    Domains). This can only register domains with .co.uk or .org suf-
    fixes (not .com). Check out whether your carefully chosen domain
    name is available at *http://www.nominet.net/whois.html* first.
    Again, print out any useful information pages. The
    FreeDomNames routine requires that you make a 2–3 minute
    phone call to set up the domain, at £1.50 per minute. There will
    also be a £5 per two years' ongoing registration free. Still, that's
    a domain for a fiver, which is a bargain. It generally takes 12–24
    hours (on weekdays) for all the registrations etc to work, after
    which go to *http://www.signup.freedomnames.co.uk/updates/* to set
    up your web space.

This service also supports FrontPage 2000 (for the more adventurous
web page designers) and will accept e-commerce.

FREE PHONE CALLS

By the time you read this, phone and cable companies will be falling
over each other offering you free calls, or a very cheap rate for all
your internet. AltaVista is proposing to charge a one-time fee of
about £30 ($50) and will not subject users to built-in banner ads
(although users will see a built-in advertising window). A similar dial-
up service in North America, Free Access, has two million users. BT
is offering a similar deal, but at a higher rate plus a monthly charge.
Telewest's Surf Unlimited will be £10 per month ($15) for all inter-
net calls using their number. It may be that, as you read this, there
are even better, cheaper or free deals available. All will want you to
use their dial-up number, browse starting at their home page and pay
attention to their advertising. But there are ways around that (see
Subvert your free ISP, page 32).

Step 2

Get a Good Idea

THINK BEYOND THE BOX

Most people start thinking about e-business in the context of an existing business, and how to put it on-line. There is nothing wrong with this – it may be what you eventually do – but it doesn't hurt to think laterally as well. For instance:

- Don't come up with a new idea, but a new business model to add to your existing business. This might be:
  - a new way of connecting purchasers and retailers
  - a new way of contacting customers
  - a new way of researching and scoping the market.

The three great advantages of new business models are:

- There are no rules, so no one can tell you 'you're doing it wrong'.

- New business models scale up more easily than expanding an existing business model. This means profit margins are potentially higher.

- You will be ahead of the field and everyone else will have to catch up.

Good examples of businesses which adopted a new business model are:

- EasyJet, which made on-line airline ticket booking easy, cheap and understandable.

- On-line car buying services, which took orders first then negotiated build deals direct with the manufacturers.

- Free ISPs, which want your retail business on-line, so they make it easy and cheap for you to be on-line.

THINK GLOBAL, ACT LOCAL

Your aspiration may be to run a global business – and the internet certainly allows you to do that. But it may be best to start with a locally-based campaign and expand from there. For instance, even the smallest town has a need for contractors, web design, word processing, database management, proof-reading, career counselling, CV production, house-letting and a variety of other services – all of which can be done over the internet or by phone and fax.

CASE STUDY 1

Valerie decided to start a house-letting business in the East of Scotland, based on the fact that the Open Golf Championship would be there. Her brother, a professional golfer, would be playing but couldn't find an affordable hotel to stay in. Valerie found him a house to rent and decided there was a market. She now has an on-line letting and property management company. However, she also spotted the fact that if the people renting from her needed a plumber, electrician, baby-sitter or chauffeur, why should they have to make a number of phone calls? And if they were foreign, they would certainly not understand the local business culture, not to mention the phone system. So she can provide all these services and more via her web site – taking a commission in the process. And why stop there? People like to eat in restaurants, want to go to movies, like to find nice pubs to visit, want to know what visitor attractions there are locally and when the trains run. Valerie's site has all these information services and the ability to make reservations if required. From a local service the site has expanded her business to the point where someone in, say, Australia can rent a property, hire a car, book flights, get the correct newspapers ordered, organise a golf game or a tennis match and – this was an especially good idea – hire a computer all set up and ready *with the client's e-mail accounts on!*

DO WHAT YOU LIKE

By which I mean – do what you love!

There may be many things you could do, but what gives you the most pleasure? If you can't do it, get additional training or partners who can.

CASE STUDY 2

Alex always wanted to grow herbal plants. He was an engineer and a keen gardener and therefore not unsophisticated when it came to the technical side, but wasn't really much of a business expert. He took the appropriate courses at the college where he worked (cheap for staff, of course), took early retirement and used his lump sum to acquire the land, buildings and stock he needed. He soon realised there was a market for herbal remedies and aromatherapy products but didn't really have the expertise to handle these aspects. So he made a deal with a nearby herbal therapist who had no desire to get into the mail order business herself, and together they now run a successful herbs-by-mail company. Further, Alex's business is a visitor attraction with a tea shop, children's play area and small display garden – all of which he can market using his web site. And he does.

FIND OUT WHAT'S NEEDED

The other great advantage of starting locally is that you can talk to business people, voluntary agencies, neighbourhood and community groups, your Local Enterprise Company (in Scotland) or Training and Enterprise Company (England and Wales), Business Link service and local authority to find out what unfulfilled needs there are – which might be business needs, communication needs or personal needs.

CASE STUDY 3

Doreen worked as a home care assistant and spent a lot of her time shopping for her customers. Now she operates a web-based service where disabled or house-bound clients e-mail her or call her answerphone to order their shopping. She orders it from local shops who pay her a commission, and they deliver it to the addresses concerned. She even negotiated on behalf of two shops who didn't have a delivery service with one who did, and now everyone is happy.

As a sideline to this she also discovered that there was a considerable amount of mail and parcel delivery between two offices in one town and a factory in another town nearby. This cost a fortune in couriers but not enough to merit acquiring a van and a driver full time. Now the grocery delivery van fills in any extra time collecting and delivering these parcels far cheaper than before. The company is happy. And it didn't take a genius in the factory – which is quite far from any shops – to realise that if a grocery van was coming to their site twice a day, it could also deliver their shopping. So now the factory workers order on-line from Doreen.

The boss of the company was so impressed with this as an example of e-business that it changed his whole outlook, and he has made a substantial investment in re-engineering his business to take account of the web. And who got a fat consultancy fee for some down-to-earth advice? Doreen.

DECIDING WHAT TO SELL

The facts are:

- books and CDs sell most – about 15% of purchases

- speciality products (chocolate, flowers, gourmet foods, greeting cards, perfume and wine) are about the same

- computer products are a close third at around 13%.

That's almost half the internet market right there. Everything else – holidays, airline seats and luxury yachts – is in the other half. That's what you're up against.

CASE STUDY 4

Al is a great blues singer. He has two CDs of his own songs, plus one made by the band he also sings with. Being low-volume sales and, let's face it, pretty unknown, he can't persuade any large retail chain to stock them. Even if he did, does he want to commit to a large pressing of hundreds of CDs to send out sale-or-return at his own risk? Of course not. That's what record companies are for. One option is to sell them on-line and have them produced in small batches as he needs them. He is quite prepared to address envelopes and stick stamps on by himself. He has two options, therefore:

1 Have his own site – fortunately, he has a daft friend who will design it for him and get it onto a free server. So far that hasn't cost him anything but time and a few beers. Any orders he receives will come to him as e-mail and he can organise the packaging and postage. But how does he receive payment? For the low volume and amounts, it probably isn't worth setting up a separate

merchant service. Fortunately, his site was partially built using ShopFactory, which comes with an order processing facility.

2   Get the CD on someone else's site – because he has a small number of items at low cost he doesn't see the economic case for taking one of those £30 a month bespoke catalogue offers. He'll never get the money back. However, zShops at Amazon.co.uk (*http://www.amazon.co.uk/*) is ideal for this. Amazon take the order, e-mail Al to fulfil it and send him payment regularly, less a handling charge.

Al took both of these options. If he hadn't had the daft friend referred to above he could have set up a basic site with one of the free ISPs and put in a link to zShops. The ISP might have considered this e-commerce contrary to their agreement and pulled his site. After all, the whole point of free ISPs is that you will be presented with adverts and opportunities to buy the things the ISP wants to sell, not someone else's products.

The other facility worth having in a site you control is the sale of other people's goods. If you buy Al's CDs you might like the other blues CDs or books about blues artists. So, there is a link to amazon.co.uk and one to CDNow – Al is registered as a reseller with both so for any CDs, books or other items you purchase through Al's site, he receives a small commission and never has to handle the goods. Now that is a worthwhile service.

SOME BUSINESS TRUISMS

Truisms can look trite, but that's because they are usually obvious and true. But pondering them can help you start and run a small business.

- **A friend or relative is not necessarily a good business partner.** It's good to have a partner to bounce ideas off, but choose one for the right reasons. Being friends is not enough and being distantly related through marriage with a common interest in ice hockey is no reason at all.

- **A successful business looks the part**. This is not an excuse to move to plush premises with state-of-the-art interior design. But at least make sure your workshop or office is clean, tidy, well-decorated and smoke-free.

- **Any business will run at a loss for the first full year**. Make sure you have enough resources to cope with this, or have not risked more than you can find. Most businesses fail due to cash flow deficit ('I'm owed lots of money but I can't collect it, so I can't buy any new stock').

- **Bargaining saves money**. I know, we're British and we don't haggle. But it's amazing how often people are willing to negotiate. Don't forget barter as well.

- **Business success requires that you love what you do**. Don't do anything just for the money. You will end up hating it (and yourself) and you will fail.

- **Don't use your professional advisers like a fire service**. Lawyers, bank managers and accountants are not there just for the bad times. A regular 'How's it going' chat and a business health checkup should be part of your routine processes.

- **Everyone is a potential customer** . . . and don't you forget it. One friend who runs a courier business tells his employees that each delivery makes them around £5 profit and a new customer costs about £50 to get. So keeping existing customers is of major importance. He tells his staff to imagine everyone they meet as having £50 emblazoned on their foreheads.

- **Fail to plan, plan to fail**. Business planning (see page 19) is difficult. There is no immediate evidence as to whether it is working or not. But a properly formulated plan will be like a road map for the next few years – business objectives, current situation, long-term goals, initial assumptions, calculated risks and regular progress monitoring should all form part of it. Be prepared to change it – you are not writing it in stone.

- **Have a formal partnership agreement**. Right at the outset, get a legal agreement together which covers initial contribution, profit and loss split, roles and responsibilities, continuation if one partner pulls out, trade mark ownership, liabilities apportionment, buy/sell options, inclusion of other partners, compensation and management functions. Too many businesses fail because the partner with sales and marketing responsibilities sees it as an excuse to spend more time on the golf course or in the pub with his 'prospects'.

- **If it's a good idea someone else will do it sooner or later**. If you wait, someone will beat you. Eventually you will have competitors. Be prepared to strike off in another direction.

- **If you borrow money, you will have to give a personal guarantee**. This may be in terms of signing your house over to the bank. Think very carefully before signing anything. *Never* borrow money from family members – you will have to face them at weddings for years to come.

- **If you train them, they'll leave**. But if you don't train them, they'll stay. Which is worse?

- **It takes a leader to start, run, and grow a business**. You can tell the difference between managers and leaders when the going gets tough. Managers go through the motions and do what they know rather than what's needed. Decisive action is key and sometimes it doesn't matter what decision is taken, as long as there is a decision. Managers agonise, leaders do.

- **Keep your job while you start up**. Think of your current employer as an additional resource in the early phases. That doesn't mean you can steal the paperclips and stationery, but use the time and space regular employment gives you to test out your business. Leave when it's obvious that you have the beginnings of a success on your hands.

- **Marketing is all**. A lot of businesses with one customer and all your time is spent supporting this one income source. But if it goes away, where do you turn to? Spread your income base widely and expand your markets all the time.

- **Back up everything every night**. One day soon your computer will crash and lose all your business information.

- **Pay yourself first**. Another obvious one? Some people put every penny back into the business. At least some of it should be a decent salary and a pension plan for you and your partners. Don't overdo it on the company cars, walnut desks and 'business' holidays, though. There is a balance to be struck. 'Lifestyle' companies don't last long.

- **There is no 'best option' for business organisation**. You will have to consider whether you want to be a sole trader, partnership, limited company or plc. You also need to consider VAT registration – the paperwork is a pain, but you do recover the VAT you pay. If you don't pay much (and you are under the VAT threshold), don't bother. But get professional advice from lawyer, accountant or both.

- **This is not your whole life**. Keep home and business separate as much as possible and don't neglect the one in favour of the other. If the business crashes you'll need all the support you can get. If it's a wild success, you'll want to share the fruits of that with someone. Keep a hobby going. Do not get too single-minded about the business. It's only one-third of your life.

- **Will it sell**? To be successful you must have a product, skill or service people want to buy. Obvious, but often forgotten in the rush to turn a hobby into a business. Remember also that times change – how many radio repair shops do you see nowadays?

- **You get the employees you pay for**. Hire the best, train them constantly and let them develop skills you don't have. Don't forget that every pair of hands comes with a free brain attached.

Step 3

Get e-mail

ADVANTAGES OF E-MAIL

Electronic mail is one of the least technically sophisticated, easiest to use and most useful aspects of the internet. And with a few modifications it can weave seamlessly into other applications such as contact databases, payment systems and web pages.

Just as the availability of easy to use spreadsheet programs in the 1970s and 1980s popularised the desktop computer, e-mail has driven the wide acceptance of the internet. The web is fun, jazzy and pictorial, but people really *use* e-mail for an actual purpose – communication.

There are numerous advantages to e-mail over other telecommunications methods:

1 If you wanted to give ten people the same message by phone it would need ten phone calls – with e-mail you can contact as many people as you like, usually by a single e-mail.

2 It is fairly instantaneous – there is practically no delay in sending and receiving e-mails, provided your server sends them instantly and the receiver reads them right away. It is certainly faster than even the fastest post or courier service.

3 A properly-worded e-mail can't be misunderstood the way a non-recorded phone call can ('But I thought you said . . .').

4 It provides a permanent record of what you sent, to whom and (if set up properly) whether they received and read it.

5 It takes the fax a logical step further – with a fax you compose a document (probably on a computer), then turn the digital information into a completely different format by printing it onto paper, reconvert it back to digital information for transmission to a receiving fax machine, where it is again converted into print-on-paper. E-mail avoids the step in the middle, and has the added

advantage that the message is in a form which can be amended and edited. A disadvantage is that hand-written signatures cannot be sent (yet!) in a form acceptable for legal purposes. Another is that a pre-existing paper document can't readily be sent by e-mail without scanning it into a computer – a process almost identical to faxing, so you may as well fax it.

6 Although the two technologies will co-exist for a while, there are still more people within reach of a fax machine than e-mail. However, the two systems are coalescing – your PC is probably capable of sending and receiving fax directly (with the right software) and for those not on e-mail, there are e-mail-to-fax programs which allow you to reach fax machines with an e-mail message.

7 Pictures can be sent by e-mail at their existing resolutions (try printing a colour photograph and faxing it!) and so can audio, video and practically any other form of information which can be digitised.

8 It is almost free – provided your ISP or OSP isn't charging for connect time, all it costs is your time and a phone call. Considering you can send one e-mail to multiple recipients, this is an incredibly cost-effective business tool.

9 Granted, e-mail is capable of abuse – anyone who is on the receiving end of '**spam**' (unwanted junk e-mails) knows how frustrating and time-wasting this can be. However, you can set up your e-mail client to filter or exclude such nonsense.

10 Best of all, e-mail can be automated in ways that other communications systems can't – you can forward e-mails to another location when you are elsewhere, set up an automatic response to say you are on holiday, notify you of e-mails received, log in from other places to receive your messages and so on.

DISADVANTAGES OF E-MAIL

The two main drawbacks to e-mail come from the opposite ends of the user spectrum – those who don't use it and those who use it too much. Every organisation with e-mail has people who won't use it, can't use it properly or aren't connected. They can't get the advantages of it, and you can't use it to best advantage with them. So make sure everyone is on e-mail and checks it regularly. It only takes a statement from the boss that all meetings will be notified by e-mail *only* – anyone who misses a meeting through wilful refusal to use e-mail won't be around long. On the other hand, in some organisations e-mail has become so popular – overused, in fact – that staff can spend entire mornings reading and responding to messages.

The answer to both of these problems is an e-mail awareness session with all employees – lay out the advantages and settle rules for its use. Some of these might be:

1   Use it! Everyone should check their e-mails three times a day.

2   Use it properly! You don't need to check every five minutes. If your computer system is on a network it may be set up to have e-mail open all the time and to 'ping' when a message is received. There is no need necessarily to read it instantly – check who it's from, what it's about and deal with it when appropriate, just as you would with a paper message someone plonked on your desk.

3   Use is appropriately! This is not an excuse to engage in gossip sessions with Mark from accounts. There is a temptation to use e-mail as the digital equivalent to hanging about over the coffee machine but it has the advantage of looking like you're working. Announce that all e-mail logs will be collected weekly and such practices will stop.

4   Make it clear that e-mail is a business tool and the contents are property of the employer, just like business letters or the company's telephone. Abuse of the latter two wouldn't be tolerated, so why should e-mail? Nobody minds the odd personal call or e-mail, but it is a privilege, not a right.

In general treat e-mail as a welcome extension to business communications and a time-saver, not as a extension to social life and a time-waster.

YOUR E-MAIL ADDRESS

There are three main ways to get an **e-mail address**.

1   Your ISP will provide you with one, which may be associated with their **domain**. For instance, a Compuserve user will have an address like *anderson@compuserve.com* (which is friendlier and

easier to remember than their previous number system, such as *654321.123@compuserve.com*).

2   There is free web-based e-mail available from many internet companies such as Yahoo, Netscape or Microsoft. These are usually advertised as 'e-mail for life' and certainly the address – *billy@yahoo.com*, for instance – never needs to change. Web-based is accessed through a browser and can be accessed from any computer – all you need is your **log-in name** (**username**) and password. This is handy for people on the move.

3   If you have your own **domain name**, and especially if you have a web site hosted by a provider, you can get an e-mail address with the domain. This may be a true **POP3** e-mail address or an 'alias' for e-mail forwarding. For instance, I use ConnectFree as my dial-up ISP. They provide me with up to five e-mail addresses of the type *bruce@freestuff.connectfree.co.uk* ('freestuff' being the sub-domain they have allocated to me, and I chose the name). This is my 'real' e-mail address. However, my web site is hosted by First-Net using a domain (fifeweb.net) I registered. They will forward any e-mail sent to *(anything)@fifeweb.net* to my 'real' address above. As far as anyone out there is concerned, they e-mail *bdurie@fifeweb.net*. I sometimes put a slightly different form of this in web pages or e-mails (*info@fifeweb.net, sales@fifeweb.net* etc) which all get sent to the same 'real' address. But from the name before the '@' sign I can tell what the source was and I can even filter them into different mailboxes.

To give two concrete examples of how this can be useful:

1   I once bought, against my better judgement, something from an on-line shop I knew would hound me with interesting purchasing opportunities for evermore, usually dressed up as something else (like marketing tips or whatever). I gave my e-mail address as *rubbish@fifeweb.net,* and set my e-mail program to block any mail to that particular address. If they are e-mailing me, they are doing so into thin air. They may have got enough 'e-mail not received' messages back to delete me from their lists. I have no idea and I don't care.

2   When setting up a web site for a client (say, Fife Lawnmowers) I will include an e-mail link to *fifelawnmowers@fifeweb.net* by which users can notify me, as **webmaster**, of any problems with the site.

I know from the incoming address that the e-mail is connected with that site and that it's something I should probably look at quickly and fix if necessary.

Small companies can use the 'five free e-mail addresses' provided by free ISPs to good effect. If you really have five employees, each can have an individual e-mail address. If it's just you, feel free to set up addresses like *sales@myplace.freething.co.uk, marketing@myplace. freething.co.uk, feedback@myplace.freething.co.uk*, and any others that make you look larger than you are. Even if you have only one 'real' e-mail address, if you have e-mail forwarding you can use addresses like *sales@. . .* or *accounts@. . .* which will all be forwarded to your single 'real' address.

POP3 and SMTP

There is a nicety to the above, however. Most modern e-mail programs and most ISPs use **POP3** for incoming mail (receiving) and **SMTP** for outgoing mail (sending). This is because POP3 accesses mail on an electronic post office or mail server and SMTP is used to communicate between a computer and a post office server. Why this matters is that if SMTP is used to receive mail, the system thinks it is communicating with another post office, not an individual computer, and *all* mail for a certain domain will come to that computer – so *john@ourplace.com* and *janet@ourplace.com* will be identical to the system and anyone will get everyone's mail. With POP3 for receiving, each individual e-mail address requires a separate log-in. John and Janet will get their own mail, not each other's.

But what if you have set up addresses like *sales@ourplace.com, info@ourplace.com* etc and they're really all just you, or you want to see them all? Simple – have all of them in your e-mail program's Accounts configuration and your e-mail client POP3 will sweep each one in turn.

Remember that the first person who downloads an e-mail message effectively prevents anyone else from getting it. So if you think this is a way to read John's and Janet's e-mails without them knowing, it won't work. (There are other ways to do that!)

Demon is one ISP which uses SMTP for both sending and receiving, which can complicate life for multiple-user domains but simplify it for a single user with multiple addresses.

INTRANETS AND NETWORKS

If you want to give everyone on your organisation's network the ability to use e-mail over the internet, you will need a **multi-user account** from your ISP. Even if you do not need that now, you may in future so check that it is an option.

If your office network already has a mail system installed for internal communication – Microsoft Mail is an example, which comes with networked Windows – this can also be used for internet e-mail. However, you will need a **server** and a **gateway program**. Installing these is a specialised task. Alternatively, if you already have an **office server**, you could install a **mail server program** on it. Each user sends and receives e-mail using (say) Outlook Express, but in fact they are interacting with the server which is actually dialling into the internet and doing the transfers via the ISP's multi-user account.

FINDING E-MAIL ADDRESSES

Mailing lists
These are dealt with below (page 53).

Directories
The only sure way to get an e-mail address is to phone someone and ask them. Daft, isn't it? There are no reliably complete e-mail directories as there are phone books. However, there are directories to which internet users can choose to post an entry. You can also use these to search for postal addresses and other contact details if they are given. The best known are Switchboard at AltaVista (*http://altavista.switchboard.com/*), People Finder at Yahoo (*http://people.yahoo.com/*), Bigfoot (*http://www.bigfoot.com/*) and Four11 (*http://www.four11.com/*). Some of these have a very US-bias and require a two-letter State abbreviation or a zip code in a certain format, but there is usually an international section for the other 5.8 billion of us.

The implication for a business is – how can anyone find your e-mail address if you don't tell them? Therefore, register with as many directories as you can, starting with the four above. Give the fullest details possible – postal address, phone, fax, URL, description of products or services if allowed. Some are divided into White Pages (personal addresses) and Yellow Pages (business addresses) and some Yellow Pages, but not all, require a payment. It is, after all, a trade advertisement. It is your decision whether the cost is worth it.

Company domains
Companies with a number of employees usually have their own

domains and give everyone an individual e-mail address (*jim@mycompany.com*, or in more formal organisations *b.simpson@ourfirm.co.uk*). Some organisations have taken the logical step of deciding (and announcing) that all e-mail addresses will be of the form *firstname.lastname@organisation.com*, so merely knowing an employee's name will give you a good chance of knowing their e-mail address.

OSPs and ISPs

If you know someone is registered with a given ISP or OSP, you can usually search for their name in that site. This is certainly true of OSPs. Incidentally, you generally need to know the *full* e-mail address of someone to reach them – the bits before *and* after the '@', unless you are with one of the OSPs like Compuserve or AOL and want to send a message to someone you know is also registered with the same system. In that case, you can get away with just using the prefix (the bit before the '@') and the domain is assumed by the internal mail system. This is just like sending an internal memo – you would address it to Sheila, Accounts, rather than use the full postal code. However, it does not apply to ISPs – *jimbo@freeserve.co.uk* can't send a message to *bimbo@freeserve.co.uk* just by sending it to *bimbo* – you need the full address.

Use your literature

You will be putting your e-mail address on all your stationery, business cards, promotional brochures, fliers, newspaper small ads, block ad in the local phone book, posters and shop window, won't you? Obvious, but you'd be surprised how many companies, both large and small, spend a fortune on print advertising of various kinds and neglect to tell the public the easiest way to contact them. Do not make the same mistake.

THE COMPONENTS OF E-MAIL

Enough of the theory – how does it all work? When you use e-mail, the following processes take place.

1 You compose a message on your computer **off-line** (not connected) using an **e-mail client** (program). You specify the recipient, whether it is to be copied or blind-copied (copied without other recipients seeing that address) and any attachments, such as a document, spreadsheet or whatever.

2 You connect to your dial-up ISP (often you can automate your e-mail client to dial up when you press 'send') and the e-mail is sent to your ISP's mail server. If you are on a network, it may be that all outgoing mail is stored until a certain time (say, four times a day) before being sent on as one large batch. Why anyone does this is a mystery, since it simply puts a delay in the system that needn't be there.

3 A certain amount of checking takes place – can it be sent, is it corrupted in any way, is the recipient's e-mail address recognisable – and it will be sent on, or sent back to you with a message explaining why it couldn't go.

4 Either right away, or after a delay (see 2, above) the mail server will calculate the fastest and/or cheapest route across the internet backbone to your recipient's ISP. It may hit thousands of computers on its way, which is why security is an important issue! (See page 101).

5 The receiving server takes the e-mail message and – if the recipient's name is recognised – stores it in the appropriate **mailbox** (in reality a folder or directory on the server where that person's e-mails go until read. Alternatively, the server may refuse to accept the message
– if it is too long (some servers have an upper size limit to prevent becoming clogged with huge files)
– if it contains 'disallowed' words (some organisations are concerned about staff accessing or receiving dubious information)
– if the address is in some way wrong
– if it contains a virus.
In these cases you will get it back with a message attached explaining why. You may get a **receipt** (a message saying it has been received) if you set your own e-mail program to ask for one.

6 When – and *only* when – the recipient chooses to access the mailbox is the message downloaded to his or her own PC. You may then get a message telling you the message has been opened and read. Usually it is deleted from the server after a few hours or days, to save storage space. But a copy resides on the recipient's PC until it is cleared out.

7 If the recipient is on a network – at a large company or a college, say – the mail will be sent on immediately and if the e-mail program is open, it will notify the user with a noise or visual signal of some sort.

8 The recipient may have set up filters to send messages to particular mail folders – sales, personal, etc or folders dedicated to individual clients, contacts or subjects.

9 The recipient can reply to your message, forward it elsewhere, store it, archive it, delete it or just plain ignore it. But at least it got there.

10 If there is a reply, the whole process happens again in reverse and you will receive it next time you log on and open your e-mail client.

E-MAIL CLIENT PROGRAMS

In order to send and access e-mail you need:

* a dial-up ISP
* an e-mail account with that ISP or another provider
* the hardware to make the connection (modem, ISDN router, LAN card etc)
* dial-up networking software
* an e-mail client – the program which makes it all work.

These were covered in Step 1. The remainder of this chapter will assume that you have Microsoft Outlook Express or a similar e-mail client. Most of them are similar in operation.

Configuring your e-mail

Your ISP will tell you the various parameters you need to connect to the mail system. In particular, you will need to know the incoming and outgoing mail boxes, your account name and any password you need to connect (Figure 1.).

COMPOSING AND SENDING E-MAIL

There is no need to be on-line (connected) when you are composing e-mails, nor to send them one at a time. You can:

* Connect to receive your e-mails, then log off and close your connection, but keep the program open so you can read messages and compose replies to send later.

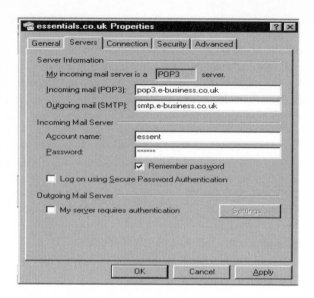

Fig. 1. Configuring your e-mail.

- Forward or reply to any program e-mails, or compose new ones. In each case, use the Send Later option to store them until you connect again.

- Send when you are ready – usually the program can be set to dial up when you send.

Sending attachments

To **attach** a file to an e-mail (send it along with the e-mail but not in the body of the message) there is a slight complication which, in practice, isn't a problem any more. However, anyone using an older e-mail program might need to know about it. The internet is a text-based system and uses seven-bit ASCII to send text. However, data files use eight-bit ASCII – try to send these by e-mail and the last bit gets cut off each packet, corrupting the data. To get round this, a protocol called UUEncode was developed. This turns data files into text-like files, which can be decoded at the other end. However, it relies on both sender and recipient knowing what they are doing.

A new standard was developed called MIME (Multipurpose Internet Mail Extensions) which can send any file format reliably so there is no need to handle attached files in any special way. This has an added advantage – e-mail programs which support MIME can read HTML formatting. In other words, your e-mail messages can be constructed like mini-web pages, with text effects like bold, italic, colour, or numbered and bulleted lists, graphics and links to web sites. This makes e-mails far more interesting and with a bit of experimentation you can send messages which are eye-catching and likely to be read.

In order to do this, make sure your e-mail program is set to send and read HTML – in Outlook Express this is in Tools, Options, Send. If you use formatting and the recipient's mail or news program does not read HTML, the message appears as plain text with an HTML file attached, which can be opened in a browser. It is worth including a statement in your messages such as 'Contains formatting – ensure your e-mail client can read HTML'.

Mailing lists

Naturally, you will be starting your own mailing lists and probably keeping them in the Address Book which came with your e-mail program. This is fine for small lists and for restricted purposes. But if you wanted to do a postal mail shot to 10,000 potential customers, you would either buy in a mailing list as a **database** (or a set of labels) or you would contract to a mailing house to do it for you.

Life is simpler on the internet. There are more than 40,000 mailing lists available free, not counting newsgroups (see below) although you may not actually get to see the e-mail addresses. They work something like a chain letter. If you find a list appropriate to your interest, sector or client group, you send an e-mail to the list, including your own e-mail address. The message gets sent to everyone already on the list and your address is added to it. In this way, the lists grow. Usually you can read previous messages and add comments to them (which are also posted to all members).

There are several things to bear in mind:

* Before engaging with a mailing list, read the **FAQ** document – this will explain the rules, such as whether advertising is allowed, whether product names can be mentioned etc. Break the rules and you will get **flamed** (sent one or more furious e-mails), removed from ever posting another message or some other sanction.

* Some lists allow paid advertising – you will have to weigh up the value of this to your business.

* Mailing lists are actually better for keeping in touch with your peers and your business area than for selling or promoting your

products. However, this may in itself be useful – like a trade newspaper.

• You have little or no control over the quality of the list – generally it will be open to anyone who wants to join. On the other hand, you're not paying per item as you would be for a mail shot or fax campaign.

There is a directory of lists at *http://www.liszt.com/* or see the Appendix.

Signature files

A useful aspect of e-mails is the ability to attach a short text (or HTML-formatted) file at the foot of every message. This is called a **signature** (or **sig**) **file**. It was originally intended as a standard paragraph including the sender's name, address, phone number etc to save typing this every time in every message. But with some ingenuity, it can be used as a valuable marketing tool. For instance, your sig file could carry a promotional message – 'Wonky Widgets – the Wildest Widgets in the World' or 'This week only – Free Widget with every ten ordered'. Use HTML formatting and you can include coloured text, graphics (such as your logo) and even a piece of music! Don't make it too large, though – nobody will thank you for making them spend ten minutes of phone bill time downloading something that just goes 'boing' at them. Make it useful and make it work for you.

If your e-mail can handle formatted text, the sig lines may look like this:

Customer Consideration Ltd – e-mail: info@customconsider.com

http://www.customconsider.com/

Tel: 0133-444-3333   Fax: 0131-555-6666

We Sell Everything Good and Everything We Sell Is Good

Customer Consideration uses ShopShelf
(http://www.shopshelf.com/)

If not, and because internet e-mail uses ASCII text (no bold or italic characters, for instance), these signature lines are often dressed up with other keyboard characters. You may see something like this:

+-+

Customer Consideration Ltd info@customconsider.com
http://www.customconsider.com
Tel: 0131-444-3333   Fax: 0131-555-6666
We Sell Everything Good and Everything We Sell Is Good
Customer Consideration uses ShopShelf
(http://wwww.shopshelf.com)

+-+

Notice the contact information and promotional text for a product
or service – including someone else's product, which they may pay
you for the privilege of including. Some e-mail programs allow multiple signature lines so you have the choice of separate business and
personal ones, or related to different areas of your business.

Signature lines and files are important when posting messages on
discussion forums. Someone might just lift the phone or look at your
web site and buy something.

Filtering messages

Your e-mail program will have a feature called something like 'message rules'. At its simplest, this is a way of blocking messages from
someone you don't want to hear from – the company which pesters
you daily or weekly with 'unbeatable' offers. Gauge your own reac-
tion to that, by the way, and don't turn into one of them!

However, it can also be used to direct incoming messages to different **folders** – like separate postboxes. Say you had various
e-mail links in your web page or different e-mail addresses on different literature – examples would be *sales@thisco.co.uk* and
support@thisco.co.uk, or *dept101@thisco.co.uk* for a special promo-
tion. These could be collected in separate folders called Sales, Support and Dept 101 which you set up for the purpose. This makes life
easier than trawling through all your e-mails to find the one from that
important customer who actually wanted to buy something.

Two other uses of Message Rules are **Autoreply** and **Forwarding**.

Autoreply
If you sent a message to a software company asking for help on
an aspect of their program, you'd be pleasantly surprised if you
got a message back almost instantly, thanking you for being in
touch and assuring you of their prompt attention to their query,
wouldn't you? You might even be fooled into thinking they had

someone reading all e-mails as they arrived and responding to them right away – not a bit of it! They're using an Autoresponder. Figure 2 shows how to set up a Message Rule (in Tools, Message Rules, Mail) which responds to any e-mail sent to *support@* ... with a simple Thank You message. This was written using Notepad and saved as thankyou.eml.

Likewise, if you were on holiday, ill or abroad, you could set up a message that said 'Back on the 24th' or something similar (but more polite and informative) that responded to *all* incoming e-mails.

But perhaps the best time-saver of all is to have your price lists, catalogues etc available as an autoresponder file and to set your e-mail to respond to any e-mail sent to *sales@* ... and with the word 'brochure' or 'price list' in the subject line with an instant piece of literature, plus a link to the URL where you have your full-colour catalogue. Now that's service!

Too cute for words

Another neat trick a colleague of mine uses is to link any e-mail from certain people to an autoresponder message rule that says 'Sorry, I'm

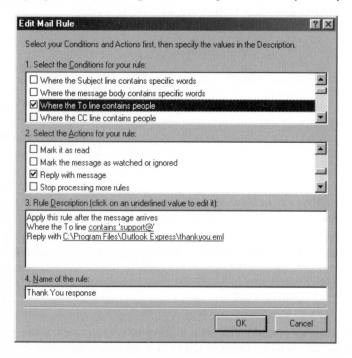

Fig. 2. Setting up a Message Rule autoreply.

a bit busy right now, but I'll reply more fully when I have time to pay the attention to your message that it deserves. Trust *Janice and the kids* are fine' – except that *Janice and the kids* is different according to the name and circumstances of the sender. One customer gets a message asking how the new caravan is performing! It's a new twist on the old salesman's personal touch. He's American – did I say?

Can't be bothered?

If you don't fancy the thought of all that autoresponding set up, your ISP may do it for you. Or, if your company runs a network, get the Network Manager to organise an automated mailbot listserver routine. Then it's his/her problem, not yours. But beware of the trap fallen into by the hated manager. He browbeat his IT person, who was leaving for a new job the next day into setting up such a thing. For a couple of weeks every e-mail in got a response saying 'Sorry, but the idle git can't be bothered with you. Go find a supplier who actually gives a monkey's' followed by a list of competitors. Ouch!

FORWARD E-MAILS WHEN AWAY FROM HOME

One of the problems with ISPs is that they tend to operate in one country – you dial a UK-only 0845 number, for instance. So how do you collect e-mails when abroad? There are three main ways:

1 Establish a new e-mail account with an OSP that has a **Point of Presence** in any country you are likely to visit. Then forward all your 'real' e-mails to that address (see below) and you can dial in with your laptop. This has the disadvantage of costing money for the OSP service on top of your ISP costs.

2 Establish a web-based 'e-mail address for life' with Yahoo, Netscape or a free ISP and forward all your 'real' e-mails to that. Web-based e-mail can be accessed through a browser, so you will still need some way of getting onto the internet. But a friend, business host, hotel or local internet café should be able to help. Your ISP may offer a service whereby your normal e-mail can be read with a browser – ask.

3 Set up an e-mail-to-fax or e-mail-to-phone service for the period you are abroad – this will send any e-mails to a specified fax number, such as the one in your hotel or at your host's office. Exam-

ples of such services are to be found at *http://www.jfax.com/* though there are others.

Alternatively, if the need is great and you can afford it, investigate Microsoft's Outlook Web Access, which allows web-based reading of standard e-mails, provided Outlook is your basic messaging system.

MAILING GROUPS

As you develop a customer base, you will want to collect the names, addresses, telephone, fax and e-mail details. This takes discipline!

*   Make it your habit to enter any new business cards into the e-mail Address Book on a daily basis.

*   Automatically add the address of anyone who e-mails you.

*   Regularly put new addresses into **Groups**. In the Outlook Express Address Book this is done using File, New Group, or by double-clicking on an existing Group name. Set up Groups for Customers, Business contacts, chums etc. You can then send Group e-mails and, at Christmas time, export them to a document to print labels for cards. And how much time did you spend last year addressing them all by hand?

*   Integrate your Address Book with other databases. If someone else in your company keeps the customer database, then work out a routine for regularly updating your (shared!) Address Book. Most e-mail address programs have an Import function. If your contact database is in some unrecognised format, export it as a Text or Comma Separated Variable file, then import it from that, remembering to match up the field names with the ones in your Address Book.

*   The point about having a shared Address Book is important. If your computers are on a network then everyone should work from the same Address Book. If you are on free-standing PCs (and laptops) then make it the responsibility of *one* person to collect all new business cards and keep a single version of the Address Book up to date, distributing a new copy weekly for those who also want it on a laptop or at home.

NETIQUETTE!

Sure, the internet (and especially e-mail) is a superb way to reach a lot of people very quickly and cheaply. But it is not a boor's charter. Abuse it – sending blatant adverts where none is welcome; becoming an e-mail pest by badgering potential customers; sending meaningless spam mail to everyone in your Address Book – and you will get Named, Blamed and Flamed.

Get a reputation as someone who does one or all of these and you will find yourself unable to join any mailing lists or subscribe to news-groups. Keep it up, and you will be on the receiving end of a vast number of e-mails all saying much the same (rude) things which will clog your system for ages and prevent you getting any work done. Remember, e-mails have to be downloaded and read in rotation. If there are 50 in the queue, each with a 2MB garbage file attached, in front of the big order you've been waiting for, you'll wait a long time.

I know one person who responds to any particularly unwelcome e-mail by replying with a frightening-looking HTML e-mail message that flashes in big red writing: 'WARNING! DANGEROUS VIRUS ENCOUNTERED! CLOSE YOUR SYSTEM NOW AND REFORMAT YOUR HARD DRIVE!' Needless to say there is no virus (who would do such a thing!) but it has probably caused a few heart failures.

The ultimate sanction is a complaint to your ISP who may well revoke your e-mail account and perhaps even pull your web site. And you'll have no one to blame but yourself.

Some basic rules are:

1 Consider carefully what you write since it might be forwarded to others. What sounded trenchant, witty and forthright at 3 am after a bottle of Chateau Plonko may come back to bite you later. You must read your e-mail before you send it – make sure your points are clearly and concisely made and spelt correctly.

2 Don't attach large files (over 50K) without getting permission from the recipient first and never attach files when posting to discussion groups. Likewise, never send web pages to a discussion group, even though most browsers have an in-built facility to do just that. Send the URL with an explanation of why you think it important, amusing, interesting etc. Send it in the form of '*http://. . .*'. Most up to date e-mail programs will recognise this as a **hyperlink**, so that one click will take the reader there.

3 Don't promote your business too obviously – like posting an advert to a discussion group – unless it is clearly an accepted practice and/or you have checked with the forum moderator (if there is one) first.

4 Don't quote back an entire message when responding – just the bit you are responding to. Some e-mail programs will automatically quote the original message when replying. Put your comments at the top of the message rather than the bottom.

5 DON'T TYPE IN ALL CAPS. This is shouting.

6 E-mail may be cheap to some, but not to everyone, so WRITE SUCCINCTLY. Sorry about the shouting.

7 Don't use cutesy acronyms like IMHO (in my humble opinion) or BTW (by the way). Use the commoner emoticons (smileys) when trying to convey a tone of voice :–) if you really must. Personally, they give me hives.

8 Make your Subject line interesting, descriptive and meaningful. Busy people only open messages which appeal to them at first glance.

9 Never forward personal e-mails to a discussion group or another party without the author's permission.

10 Turn off e-mail formatting when posting to a discussion group – a lot of programs can't handle it – and limit lines to 65–70 characters, otherwise some e-mail programs will wrap the text at the wrong place or not wrap it at all.

ORGANISE YOUR E-MAIL FOR MARKETING

Setting up a web site is covered in Step 4, but e-mail plays a valuable role in promoting that site, and as a marketing tool in its own right. Some of the material covered in this section should be referred to again after Step 4.

Push e-mail

E-mail is an example of **push** technology – in other words, you send it out *to* people rather than wait for them to find it by themselves.

Leaving aside the subject of what your web site consists of until Step 4, think first about what will get people to it.

1 Establish a regular newsletter by e-mail and invite people to subscribe to it. This is a valid way of collecting e-mail addresses and you are then justified in e-mailing them regularly. It's not spam if they ask for it, but make it easy for them to unsubscribe as well.

2 Make your newsletter different from others out there. Think up something you as a customer or person in that business sector would like to know. It could be as daft as the latest industry jokes (How many Chartered Sewage Engineers does it take to change a light bulb? Answer at *http://www.ourstuff.co.uk/icse/jokes/how-many.html'*).

3 If you change or update your web site regularly (which you *must!*) send out a weekly or monthly e-mail newsletter to say so. Make sure a visitor to your site can request this. If you do send it out as a bulk e-mail, put *all* the recipients in the BCC (Blind Carbon Copy) field, otherwise everyone will know everyone else's e-mail and you will have infuriated your customers, given your competitors a freebie and broken the terms of the Data Protection Act in the UK plus goodness knows how many laws elsewhere. You could probably go to prison in Turkey, which you wouldn't enjoy. If you would rather entrust this to a mailing list service there are many, including eGroups (*http://www.egroups.com/*) and Topica (*http://www.topica.com/*) (both free, but they insert their own advertising) and BusinessMail UK (*http://www.businessmail.co.uk/*).

4 ISSN numbers lend credibility. Just as books have ISBN numbers, you can register an e-mail newsletter or e-zine with the US Library of Congress and get an International Standard Serial Number (ISSN). And it's free. This gives credibility and may get your publication onto a few more lists. More details are at *http://lcweb.loc.gov/issn/e-serials.html*.

5 Promote your newsletter in mailing lists and newsgroups (if you're allowed to!). Make it a valuable service to interested people.

6 Give away free information – 'Latest reviews on new window washers' or 'Gardening tips month by month, day by day' or 'What to do and where to go in Skelmersdale – July issue' – but make people visit the web site to get it.

7 Consider different language versions – the web is very English-biased and potential customers in other countries may not be getting any information from your competitors, because they can't be bothered translating it into Danish or Swahili. If you have any facility for languages, the chances are you know something about the country concerned and can make a decent guess at what might interest them. Otherwise, choose a country or language group, find a relevant student from that country at the local college or university and get translating. And here's a free business idea – if there's a newsletter you particularly like or find useful, offer to translate it in exchange for an advert for your product, a link to your web site, the chance to say something about your service each month etc. There are automated translation services around, like AltaVista's Babelfish (*http://babelfish.altavista.digital.com/*).

8 Haunt other people's discussions – apart from mailing lists and newsgroups there are bulletin boards and some web sites run discussion pages. OSPs like Compuserve have **forums**, as do many ISPs. Do not go barging in with out-and-out adverts, but if someone has expressed a desire to know more about Spode pottery and you happen to sell Spode pottery, suggest gently that there is good, free information on your web site (and make sure there is!) after which they might linger and buy something. If you sell bespoke software, get into the appropriate discussion groups and when there is a suitable opening, suggest that you had to solve that problem, address that hardware issue, solve that conflict, would anyone like to see the solution in action, happy to send you a demo, here's the web site. Treat it like you would conversation at a dinner party – 'So where do you live, Harry?' 'Leicester.' 'Oh. Want to buy an insurance policy?' Wouldn't work, would it? And you won't be invited back. The most important discussion groups are listed in sites given on pages 133–5.

9 Get into e-zines. There are hundreds of electronic magazines out there which will happily take money off you for an advert. But for free they may review your latest book, 'print' a letter from you, list your web site if it offers something new or different, accept a submission on a relevant subject into which you can slip a reference to your site. There is a list of e-zines maintained at *http://www.meev.net/~johnl/e-zine-list* and you can submit articles using a variety of **automated submission** processes (see pages 76–80 and the Appendix).

10 Start your own newsgroup. Just as there are 40,000 mailing lists, there are 40,000 newsgroups. Look at *http://www.dejanews.com* for a near-complete listing. So does the world need another one? Maybe, if a particular interest or niche isn't served. If your idea is good enough, you may persuade your ISP to set it up and maintain it.

11 When posting to a newsgroup, include a sig file with a link to your URL (see page 54) just as you would with an e-mail.

12 Use correct English. This is so important it deserves a special section of its own.

SPEAK PROPER!

Just because e-mail is an informal medium and web sites are colourful, that doesn't mean you can let the standards of written English slip. Particularly if you are sending promotional or sales-type e-mails, or producing an on-line newsletter or e-zine, you need to take pains not to ignore the basic rules of spelling, punctuation, syntax and grammar.

In your business life you would not be impressed if you received a letter from another organisation which had misspellings and infelicities of expression, so bear in mind that others will judge you the same way. There are any number of lovingly-crafted and gorgeously-designed web sites out there – some of them from major companies – shot through with poor spelling and awful constructions.

There are some basic rules. The most famous are those quoted by George Orwell when he wrote the in-house style guide for *The Economist* a number of years ago, and they still hold true (*Politics and the English Language*, 1946). These are:

1 Never use a metaphor, simile or other figure of speech which you are used to seeing or hearing.

2 Never use a long word where a short word will do.

3 If it is possible to cut out a word, always cut it out.

4 Never use the passive where you can use the active.

5 Never use a foreign phrase, a scientific word or a jargon word if you can think of an everyday English equivalent.

6 Break any of these rules sooner than say anything outright barbarous.

To these I would add my own four *bêtes noirs* (see, I just broke Rule 5):

7 Beware the 'grocer's S'. This is the increasingly-common habit of apostrophising plurals. The plural of video is videos, not video's and PC's means 'belonging to the PC'. However, 'it's' means 'it is' and 'its' means 'belonging to it'. 'Who's' is short for 'who is' and 'whose' means 'belonging to whom'.

8 Watch the special characters. Try to avoid exclamations (!) except for real emphasis (FREE!). Don't use semicolons(;) and colons(:) unless you are confident of their use: colons (like that one) introduce; semicolons (like that one) separate. The ellipsis (three dots) used to indicate a sentence tailing off can be very irritating, especially if . . .

9 A preposition (like 'with') is a bad thing to end a sentence with.

10 And never start a sentence with a conjunction, like 'and'.

If you find yourself saying something clumsy, there is usually another way to express it.

Use a decent dictionary. Do *not* rely entirely on spell-checkers – they could have wrongly-spelt words in, and can't distinguish between correctly-spelt but wrongly-used alternatives (like 'can't' and 'cant').

There are many books which deal with grammar and punctuation and with written business English. If you genuinely have problems with literacy, ask your local college or employment service for details of adult literacy courses. As a last resort, *always* have someone else read anything you produce for sense and for mistakes. Even the most competent of writers do this.

Step 4

Get a Web Site

If you have an existing web site the first section may still be of interest to you. It contains ideas and concepts which your current site may not incorporate.

JARGON

First there are some definitions to get out of the way. When you connect to the internet for web or e-mail, you are using a **dial-up** to an **internet service provider** (**ISP**) who provides a **host** service on a **server** (a physical computer where your web site, e-mail post-boxes etc are kept). When you connect to e-mail, any new messages are downloaded to your **e-mail client** (the program you use to access e-mail) on your **client PC** (the one on your desk). When you access any web site, whatever its **domain** (the name it is known by, like microsoft.com or fifeweb.net), your **browser** (the program which displays web pages, like Netscape or Internet Explorer) temporarily downloads these pages so you can view them. If you have your own web site, you will **upload** it to the **host**, probably using **file transfer protocol** (**FTP**) so it resides on the **server**, where everyone can view it.

BUILDING YOUR OWN WEB SITE

There are many advantages to building a web site from scratch. These include:

* The ability to determine and control its appearance – this may not be possible if your current site is supplied as part of a dial-up or 'free' package.

* The possibility of adding interactive elements and e-commerce (which some web site hosts won't allow – including the 'free' ISPs associated with high street stores).

- Integration of on-line catalogues and shopping cart systems from the outset, rather than shoe-horning them in later.

- Choice of interesting effects and technologies (animation, shock-wave, audio, video and others).

- Integration of discussion forums, on-line customer support.

- You can exercise control over your own domain – move it to another server if you are unhappy or get a better deal, add elements to it, update it regularly and so on.

The disadvantages are:

- You have to do it yourself, or get someone else to do it for you.

- You, or your web designer, are going to have to invest in the e-commerce software. That is an extra expense.

- You have the responsibility for keeping the catalogue, price list etc up to date.

- You have to do stock control, order processing, posting or dispatching the orders.

If you have an existing web site there is no reason why you can't have a second, custom-built site elsewhere with links between them. They don't need to reside on the same server or with the same host.

ADDING TO AN EXISTING WEB SITE

Among the things you can add to an existing web site are:

- electronic shop-front or catalogue
- payment systems
- forms for customer data collection
- chat rooms
- forums or message board
- links to other sites
- additional pages or sub-webs
- database integration.

WHAT IS YOUR WEB SITE FOR?

You may have heard, or been told at an internet marketing seminar, that the web is the royal road to riches. Set up the right web site with e-commerce fully enabled and you can sit back while the millions roll in – and you won't have to do a hand's turn.

Anyone who says that is a liar, a fool or a fraud. Or a business consultant hired by the local chamber of commerce looking for extra victims.

Granted, your web site is a shop window to millions of potential customers, but:

- they won't all see it
- of those who do, a vanishingly small percentage will actually interact with it
- of those, a minuscule number will buy anything.

If that sounds dismal, look at it another way:

- even if only one per cent of people who find your web site interact with it in any way for more than ten seconds, *and*
- even if only ten per cent of them take it seriously enough to make any sort of enquiry, *and*
- even if only ten per cent of those actually buy something

then you have to get it in front of 10,000 people to make one sale. Or one million people to make a hundred sales. But if everyone who finds your site buys something, you have a success on your hands. Also, if everyone you sell to comes back for another purchase or more information, you have the beginnings of a loyal customer base.

Therefore, your web site should be:

- well known
- attractive
- easy to interact with
- constantly offering something new
- 'sticky' – people stay, interact and come back.

The trick is getting them there in the first place – with 400 million web pages to look at, who's going to look at yours? Nobody, if they don't know it exists. And they won't stay if they don't like it. Here are five hints to help solve these problems.

HINTS

Hint 1: Watch your speed

Site speed is the time (in seconds) needed for a user to download and view your start page at 28.8Kbps using a dial-up connection. Many people use 56K modems, ISDN or leased lines, but a lot do not. So design your site for the lowest common denominator. Any more than ten seconds and you'll lose them. If your page is slow to download, cut down the graphics, clever **Java** and dynamic HTML effects, or use a **gif** or **jpg** optimiser to compress your graphics and reduce download time. Good graphics programs allow you to optimise graphics (static and animated) for fast loading, often at the expense of quality. But does your gif logo need to be in 16 million colours when 16 will do? It will be smaller, faster and probably just as effective.

Hint 2: Watch the road

Site navigation must be easy, logical, intuitive and consistent. Mouse-overs, rollovers and image-swapping help and are acceptable if:

- they don't make the loading time too high
- the effect is consistent, not like a fairground
- there are no broken links, the main turn-off for casual browsers.

Check your links often to make sure the sites or pages haven't gone away or been moved.

Hint 3: Image is all

This is where a professional designer can help – not a web designer, but someone with an eye for colour, shape and form. Your web's image should reflect the nature, function, purpose and intended audience of your business, both visually and professionally. It must also be functional. The most successful sites work well, load fast and have an understated, quality look. Never use more than two type faces on any one page and if possible keep this consistent throughout the site – a common combination is a **serif font** (like Times New Roman) for headings and a non-serif font (Arial, Helvetica etc) for body text. Remember also that now everyone will have your favourite Alaska ExtraBold Italic loaded on their own PCs, so stick with the common ones given above. **Font size** is important too – pick one large enough to read but small enough to fit – using a bright coloured font against a dark background (or vice-versa) you can often get away with a smaller font size.

Hint 4: Get them in and hang on to them

'**Site Pull**' is your web's ability to attract visitors, but '**stickiness**' is a measure of how long they stay around and how often they come back. The best attraction is often a forum whereby visitors can communicate with you and each other. Does your site sell cars? Set up a discussion page on new models or classic marques. Are you dealing in antique antimacassars? Have a forum for like-minded aficionados. Into comics? Give them (and yourself) a chance to rave about the latest X-Men. Lawyer? Provide a message board where clients and other lawyers can swap news about bits of legislation.

Hint 5: Push your site

'**Site push**' technology allows you to 'push' your products or services to your visitors. It works if it isn't too intrusive or unwelcome, but it can still be quite aggressive. The commonest 'push' is a **listbot** service where you offer visitors a product, service or freebie in return for their e-mail address. This allows you to generate a client database and gives you a valid excuse for e-mailing them – it isn't spam if they have requested it.

Step 5

Get a Domain Name

GET A DOMAIN NAME

Your domain name (which you will have to register) is the heart of your internet identity. It is your brand for online activities and is unique to you. In technical terms a domain name is an alias. Computers use **internet protocol (IP)** numbers to locate each other on the internet, of the form 127.123.456.789, but these are hard to remember and hardly as user-friendly as *www.shoeshop.com* or whatever you have chosen. When you type *www.shoeshop.com* into a web browser or send e-mail to *fred@shoeshop.com*, the **domain name system (DNS)** translates this into the IP numbers used by the internet and connects you. It's analogous to having a postcode, but calling your house The Laurels, Farthingale Close, Ennytown. It can also be used as part of your e-mail address (*harry@www.shoeshop.com*) to reinforce your online branding.

REGISTER A DOMAIN NAME

If you know what you want your domain name to be, you can register it and join the other four million domain name owners. If you are not ready to go on-line with a web site just yet, you can reserve a domain, thereby protecting your internet brand until it is ready to use. Do not delay – domain names disappear fast, either because someone else has the same idea and gets in first, or because someone will speculatively register it, along with lots of other names – hoping to sell it on later. This is known as **domain name warehousing** and is increasingly common. If you have an internet service provider (ISP) or web hosting company they will provide you with the technical information you need when you register your domain, in order to 'point' it at their computers.

FIND OUT IF YOUR DOMAIN NAME IS AVAILABLE

For a *.com* domain, got to Network Solutions (*http://www.network
solutions.com/*) who will tell you if the name is available, and if not,
suggest alternatives. Other search services are Ask Reggie
(*http://askreggie.com/* and use the International Search for .co.uk etc.)
and Internic (*http://www.internic.net/*) which is the international
domain naming body. A search will also tell you who owns, hosts and
registered the domain (see Figure 3). They also maintain a list of reg-
istrars who can register on your behalf. Some of them may have special offers or deals. Just to take one example, Easyspace
(*http://www.easyspace.com/*) were charging at the time of writing:

.com – $25 per year
.net – $25 per year
.org – $15 per year
.co.uk – £5 per year
.org.uk – £5 per year.

Prices include InterNIC registration fees and a free e-mail account.

To register a .co.uk domain, go to Nominet (*http://www.nic.uk/*), a
non-profit making company which only registers UK-based companies, organisations and individuals. If you are not in the UK, find a
registrar based in your country that you can trust. It will be easier to
deal with them on the phone if everything doesn't go according to
plan.

Your ISP may register your name for you and charge you the
appropriate fee. ConnectFree (*http://www.connectfree.co.uk/*) will provide free registration for a domain name of your choice for .co.uk
and .org names (actually, it costs a three-minute phone call at £1.50
per minute plus £5 every two years). Their site includes a search facility to determine if the domain name is free. They will charge you £25
if you subsequently move the domain name to another host.

Bear in mind that OSPs and some ISPs, especially the free ones,
will only give you names that are subdomains of their own
(*jones.freeserve.co.uk* or *smith.compuserve.com*) and may require you
to take advertising from them or their associates on your web site.

Most registration services have an on-line facility, so have a credit
card handy – this is an e-business in its own right.

CHOOSING YOUR DOMAIN NAME

Letters, numbers and hyphens can be used but you cannot begin or end a domain name with a hyphen. So *my-site.com* is fine, but *-mysite.com* is not. Spaces, apostrophes ('), exclamation marks (!) and underscores (_) are not allowed in web addresses – *jim's_great site!.co.uk* would fail for all four reasons. However, you can have some special characters in file names: *mysite.com/start_here/htm* would be OK if your server allows it – some do, some don't.

A web address can be up to 63 characters long including the dot and the three or more characters of top-level domain (.com, .net, .org etc).

The .com, .net, .org, .co.uk and .plc suffixes

The **.com**, **.net** and **.org** domain suffixes indicate 'global' domains because they are not affiliated with any country. Anyone from anywhere can register a .com, .net or .org domain. You can register as many as you wish, as long as you pay the fees. These are 'top-level domains' in the **Domain Name System**. **Country-code domains** (also called **international web addresses**) are specific to individual countries – like *.uk* for the UK and .de for Germany (Deutschland). There are 191 countries which accept registrations but each has its own registration requirements – some country codes are restricted and you would have to meet strict local residence, business registration, tax, or trademark guidelines in order to register. Other country-code domains are unrestricted (like .com) and allow anyone, from anywhere, to register in their domain on a first come, first served basis. This is the case in over 80 countries – so anyone can register your company or brand name in the country-specific domain. Large companies spend several thousand pounds on 'global registration', meaning their domain is registered everywhere in every possible combination as well as the original *ourname.com – ourname.org, ourname.co.au, ourname.net.fi* etc. It's probably worth it – getting back the rights to your name can be costly and time-consuming, even if you understood the legal system in the country in question, and sometimes impossible, as any number of the world's largest companies have learned. Their lawyers are happy, though. (See Your Domain Name is Valuable, below.)

Domains ending in *.co.uk* signify a UK-based company, but there is no necessity for you to be a registered company or to be in the UK. However, it is one of the easiest domain suffixes to get. Likewise, anyone may register domains as .com, .net, and .org. A lot of business web addresses end in .com because this suffix has become the one most closely associated with businesses and looks smarter and more global than .co.uk.

Domains registered as *.plc* must be PLCs – you will have to provide evidence in the form of a Company Registration Number or similar documentation and demonstrate that you are entitled to use the name. Other such as *.edu, .ac* and *.gov* are reserved for special purposes (education, academic and government) and the likes of us can't get them.

http://www

The *www.* or *http://www* parts are not part of your domain name. However, they are part of another type of internet address used on the web called a universal resource locator (URL) which determines the exact location of a specific resource on the internet such as a specific web page, computer, or database. The way to think of this is like the name of a shop – Big Boots could be the trading name of a shoe business anywhere, but Big Boots, High St Walthamstowe is an actual shop. There is no real need to have www. before your domain name to identify your web site, but it is typical as it lets people know it is an actual web address with content. However, what you register is the domain without the www. (unless your domain is *www.com,* of course, but that one's taken!).

HOSTING YOUR DOMAIN AND WEB SITE

Every web site must be physically on a host computer. In addition there are **domain name hosts** connected to the internet which translate URLs into the numerical IP addresses used by the internet and direct browsers to the host where your web site resides. When you register or reserve a domain name, it is recorded on a domain name host. When you sign up with an internet service provider (ISP) or web hosting service, or if your organisation has its own host servers, you will upload your web site to their computers and give them permission to hold your domain name. The domain name host directs any browser to the IP address of that computer. The implication of this is that you can change your ISP or move your web site to another computer and retain the domain name – there is a process of transferring domains between hosts which involves you giving permission for the new host to use the IP 'tag'.

YOUR DOMAIN NAME IS VALUABLE

If you are determined to have the domain name of your choice and someone else owns it, go to Target Domain (*http://www.targetdomain.com/*) and see if it's available. Some bright spark wanted $1,000 for *durie.com*. I can live without it, thank you.

You can also sell a domain name you own. But if you register domain names for the purpose of selling them on, be careful. There have been recent judgements in the UK and USA that copyright carries over onto the net. For every genius who has made a fortune out of *elvis.com* or *wallstreet.com* there is some other poor soul being dragged through the courts by Pepsi or McDonalds. They may choose to pay your exorbitant asking price rather than their lawyers' exorbitant fees, or they may choose to make an example of you. To them, it's only money. It could be your house.

Retain any certificates you receive and print any e-mails the registrar sends you. These may be required if there is ever a dispute over ownership.

Make sure you actually end up owning the domain name. Some companies act as intermediaries whereby they own the name but allow you to use it. If it proves to be very popular they may ask for a high fee for you to continue.

Above all, *always pay the fee*. If you let your annual or two-year registration lapse, one of the many sharks swimming in this ocean may snap it up instantly. They have software which trawls for lapsed and available domain names and instantly bags it for them. You should receive reminders in time.

Step 6

Get Visitors

ATTRACT VISITORS TO YOUR WEB SITE

Owning a web site can feel a bit like running a beachwear shop in the Sahara – nobody comes to it and if they did they probably wouldn't want to buy what you sell. The trick to web sites is not how good they look, how technically clever they are or how well they match the objectives of the owner (although all these things are crucial). You also have to build awareness, traffic and stickiness.

Now imagine a grotty little one-page web site, black text on a white background, no images and a single form in the middle saying 'type in your address and we'll send you a cheque for £100'. If it genuinely did that, rest assured it would get into the papers, be featured on TV and radio, discussed in all the internet magazines and be the main topic of conversation up and down the land. It would get millions of visitors. Combine that with something that guarantees you, the web site owner, £200 from everyone who gets a £100 cheque from you, and you're a billionaire in no time.

Real life is rarely that simple, of course, but it serves to underline the point that unless you can get people to know about your site, attract them to it, hold them long enough to decide to part with some cash and come back to do it all again (which is what stickiness is) you may as well be selling lilos in the desert. You will end up putting as much effort into promoting and nurturing your site as you did into its design and creation, which is the main reason all these gorgeous looking sites fail to make an impression – they are put together by people who love putting together web sites and who don't give any thought to building an audience or don't know how.

DRIVE TRAFFIC TO YOUR WEB SITE

There are ways to ensure people know about and visit your site and they fall into four categories:

- obvious but expensive
- cheap and why didn't I think of that

- don't bother
- sheer low cunning.

OBVIOUS BUT EXPENSIVE

Run a TV ad during the World Cup. OK, you probably won't, but *egg.com* (the internet banking arm of the Prudential) and AOL did. Fine, they can afford it.

CHEAP AND WHY DIDN'T I THINK OF THAT?

Use search engines

AltaVista, Yahoo, Lycos, Excite and the rest are the single major source of traffic and referrals for most web sites. They also have the benefit of being free. Most search engines and directories have a 'Submit your URL' link somewhere on the main page. Work out a description of your site in 12 words and a longer one (say 50) then write a list of keywords which describe your site and which you think may attract visitors (not always the same thing). For instance, a garage in Glamorgan might use *garage, car, cars, petrol, petrol station, filling station, Glamorgan, Wales, oil* and others. Who knows whether someone will be browsing for sites about oil exploration in Wales, turn up this site from the keywords and drop in to fill up next time? There are also automated submission engines and paid submission services. See Don't Bother, below, for the downside of this.

The three most important things are:

1 Give each page on your site a detailed and specific title.
2 Use **meta tags**.
3 Submit to the important search engines.

You can drive traffic to your site at zero cost other than your valuable time. Of course, you can submit your URL to hundreds or thousands of sites by submitting to a **link service**, or have one of the paid-for **submission services** do it for you. But in fact almost all your traffic will come from a few search engines. A top ten ranking in a major search engine like AltaVista, Lycos, or Infoseek will generate far more hits than an expensive banner ad. Over 95% of the search engine traffic to most web sites comes from the 15 major search engines. Read Make Your Web Pages Search Engine Friendly, below, then submit your URL to the engines listed on page 132, the 'must submit' search engines.

Make reciprocal links

If you find a site you like, respect and think relevant, put a link to it in your site. Then e-mail the people concerned and point out what you've done and why, so would they mind doing the same (if they like your site, of course). Bear in mind that just because your web site sells opera glasses, you don't just want links to other opera glasses sites – in fact you may not want any at all, since they're the competition. But you certainly want to be on the site that lists all opera glasses retailers. Also, people who buy Volvos tend to buy tennis racquets. Fact. Think what else your prospective visitors may want that you don't offer, and where else they might be browsing. If they do macramé, will they also buy organic apples? Are people who visit the sites of local theatre companies the sort who will buy your prints of early cinema posters? If they like to look at pictures of trains, are they candidates for your information pack on getting out more?

There is evidence that a higher percentage of web traffic comes from links even than from search engines. And since some search engines rate a given site according to how many other sites link to it, this can help your rankings.

It's not a bad idea to have a page of links in your site, since visitors will respect and pay more attention to sites they feel have been personally selected for usefulness.

Web rings

Web sites can be organised into loose confederations of like-minded or similar-subject 'rings' which may also include advertisers. Their great merit is that they cut down browsing time – anyone into Tolkein will probably join The One Ring (yes, it's really called that) and if your site is relevant enough to get included they may visit you too.

Discussion lists, newsgroups and e-zines

These are dealt with in more detail in the Appendix but the basic rule is not to do anything too overtly promotional. Being helpful and informative will do wonders for your credibility: ('Re the discussion of 10/2/99 – in fact, the Ju87D-1 Stuka was 3,484 lbs heavier than the Ju87A-1 with a wing area of 0.368 sq ft smaller. I have some good pictures of both on my site *www.oldbombers.com/stuka*').

Traditional marketing

Don't forget the basics – use personal networks, always put your web site URL and e-mail on business stationery and cards, and don't rule out normal promotional materials such as fliers and small ads in the local free papers. If you sell books, put your URL and e-mail on bookmarks. Get on local radio to talk about some humorous aspect of the internet, or some other subject close to your heart, and plug your site mercilessly. Write to your newspaper about some burning issue of the day – wheelie bins is always popular – and get your URL in the letter or alongside your name at the bottom. Give a prize to every hundredth person who visits or takes your e-mail newsletter, and make it a bottle of wine, box of chocolates or book of some kind with your URL emblazoned on it.

DON'T BOTHER

Site awards

These mean very little (you get them by just asking, in the main) and they can look awfully down-market and tacky. If your site is any good, it's going to get noticed and win one of the really prestigious ones, like a High Five, which don't take submissions. In any case awards don't signify much to normal people or to customers (you won a what? Never heard of it) and if you fill your home page with dozens of throw-away award logos it will look like a hiker's back-pack. Try for one or two well-respected, relevant awards dealing with your interest area (antiques, books, food, engineering etc).

Banner ad programmes

Oh, all right, if you must. Consult page 112 for more detail, but bear in mind that if every banner exchange worked, every site would be full of banner ads and nothing else. However, most of the big name sites do it, so you won't lose credibility and it needn't cost anything. Some banner ads can be tied to affiliate programmes which may earn you some extra income. Once your site is really pulling in visitors, you can start selling your page space to others, so you may as well find out how it works.

Paid site submission services

With a few honourable exceptions (such as Submit-It) most of these are a scam. If there was any truth to a claim like 'For a mere £99.99 you can get into the top ten of all the major search engines' then everybody would be doing it and every site would be in the top ten. See the logical fallacy here?

SHEER LOW CUNNING

Make your web pages search engine friendly

At the top of every web page there will be **hidden tags** (called meta tags) which carry information about the page. These can be used to send keywords and description to search engines. You can add or alter these by editing your page in HTML form, or your web page creation program may allow you to add them using a dialogue box.

If you see a site that receives a high ranking, View the Source (the HTML) and simply copy and paste meta tags which appear to work, amending them to suit your own page and site (such as adding your company name).

If you are not comfortable with HTML, there are programs which will generate meta tags for you. One which does this – and also submits your pages to search engines – is WebPosition Gold (*http://www.webpositiongold.com/*). There is a free trial version which works with three of the top ten search engines for 30 days after which you can download the full version for $149 (about £100). You may also wish to subscribe to the free MarketPosition Newsletter which has techniques and tips on improving your search engine rankings.

As an example of what meta tags look like, I have copied these from the WebPosition Gold page itself.

```
<title>WebPosition Gold Search Engine and Web promotion
Software - lowest prices on the web</title>
<head>
<meta name="keywords" content="promotion, software, mar
keting, advertising, WebPosition, Web Position, First, Place,
FirstPlace, rankings, search, engines, submission, place-
ments, positions">
<META NAME="DESCRIPTION" CONTENT="WebPosition Gold.
Improve search engine rankings and bring new traffic to
your Web site. Download a FREE Trial Version today!">
</head>
```

Send on-line press releases

You can generate interest in your site, business idea, products or service by telling thousands of people via online press release services. Among the free ones are: Comitatus *(http://www.comitatusgroup.com /pr/index/htm)*, PRweb *(http://www.PRweb.com)*, M2 PressWire *(http://www.m2.com.M2_PressWIRE/index.html)* and Webaware *(http://www.webaware.co.uk/netset/text/).*

Submit articles

E-zines need articles. So why don't you write them? Find out your favourite or most relevant e-zines and offer them articles on topics near to your business area or main interest. There are over 300,000 on-line newsletters and e-zines covering every topic under the sun. Almost all of them rely on contributors and they need experts (like you) to give them articles, advice, tips, good URLs etc. Your submission could be as little as a few paragraphs or as much as a whole page. There is rarely any payment, but what is it worth to have your name, company, e-mail address and web site URL listed?

Alternatively, the sites listed below will take submissions and automate the process for you. You post your article on the site, set up an autoresponder to send the article automatically to anyone who will guide people to your articles. Among the best are: Articles (*http://216.147.104.180/articles/submit/*), e-Zine Articles (*http://www.ezinearticles.com/add url.htm*), Idea Marketers (*http://www.ideamarketers.com/*) and Web Source (*http://www.web source.net/articlesub.htm*). Others are listed in the Appendix, page 132.

Step 7

Know Your Visitors

TRACKING YOUR VISITORS

At this point you will have:

- most of the resources you need
- some idea of what you are selling, whether products or services or both
- e-mail, and the ability to use it for marketing and selling
- a web site of some description which people can visit
- a domain name which establishes your on-line brand identity
- some visitors to your site.

You now need to build up your own electronic mailing list. You will also want to know what page or aspect of the site visitors visit most, stay at for longer or use to make a purchase. In other words:

- Who are they?
- What do they like when they visit?
- What do they do when they visit?

Traditional methods

Advertisers often try to track customer responses by surveys or other inexact methods. It is difficult to gauge the response to, say, a newspaper advertisement since there is no absolute count of how many readers saw the ad, for how long or if they made purchases or purchase decisions based on the ad. It may be necessary to employ a telesales organisation or a survey company to help. This is:

- expensive
- slow
- unreliable (customers can't remember and don't really care where they learned about your product).

Web methods

But in the wonderful world of the web there are some very straightforward ways to gather this information. What's more, the customers won't even know they are being tracked. Use the right methods and tools and you can find out:

* how many people visited your site in a given period
* where they came from (another web site linked to yours, a search engine etc)
* how long they stayed
* what they browsed
* what browser and network they are using

If you also ask them to complete a simple registration form, you can tell a new visitor from a returner.

Why you need to know
This information is essential for:

* your own marketing (so you can target both high-potential customers and those who don't buy anything)
* site improvements
* selling space to advertisers
* knowing which links, banner ad campaigns etc are working for you.

Web-site **tracking** software can gather much more (and more detailed) information than any traditional methodology.

What you need to know
There are two types of tracking software. The first goes back to the early days of the web. Each time someone loads a page, clicks on a thumbnail graphic to show a larger picture, downloads a file, video clip or audio track, accesses a database or fills in a form, a request goes to the host computer to send information and commands to the visitor's computer. Naturally, the host computer can log all of this if set up to do so.

HITS ARE NOT VISITORS

A **hit** is counted each time a visitor clicks on part of the site, and for each graphic or link on a page. Loading a page with five graphics on it registers as five hits. For instance:

- a visitor gets to your site (one hit)
- clicks on three different pages (three hits)
- plays a short audio clip (one hit)

- clicks a link to another site and comes back to yours (one hit)
- clicks on another page before leaving (one hit)

that is seven hits. If each page visited has three graphics, that will be another $6 \times 3 = 18$ hits making 25 in all. But it's just one visitor. So those 1,000 hits a week your counter registers may in reality only be 40 visitors. There are various calculations for translating hits into visitor numbers, but you can't be sure.

Usually some **logging** software is available on the server which you can access. If not, free software is widely available to do this and, to be fair, it does give a general idea of the site's traffic and can indicate trends (there more hits on a Monday or at the end of a month, for instance). The data is saved in **log files** which can be viewed, saved or printed out. Some tracking reports are in database format software, so they can be analysed easily.

There is also **hit-rate tracking** software which gives more detailed information – what browser a visitor uses, what site the visitor came from, at what modem speed and via what type of internet access account (.com, .gov, .org etc).

The software may also track error messages which can tell you that at certain times the site gets overloaded or the server can't cope.

But even with this additional qualitative data, hit rates provide vague information.

START WITH A FREE SERVICE

Many companies will give you a free hit counter, tracking software, reporting system and other analysis tools. Often, this is all hosted on their server and a link sends the information from them to you. Why do they do this? Because they can sell the information on your visitors to other internet marketing agencies or use it for their own advertisers. Note that a counter can be hidden as well as in plain sight.

Hitometer, available at Netscape's Web Site Garage (*http://websitegarage.netscape.com/*) is one of these. The free version has an extensive choice of counters, and limited reporting of URL statistics, such as daily, weekly and monthly hits, visitor's browser, referral information, search engine used and visitor loyalty/frequency. Essentially, you paste a few lines of HTML into your page and receive online and e-mail reports.

Another is Web-Stat (*http://www.webstat.com/*) which has a free 30-day demo and a full registered version at $5 (about £3) per month.

USE A FORM TO GET WHAT YOU WANT

The information you really want (names and e-mail addresses) is anonymous unless provided voluntarily. The best way to get this is by asking visitors to complete a form. Most modern web design packages have the ability to construct forms which send the information to you by e-mail or write it to a database. As well as 'who are you' information you can also ask for useful demographics such as:

- income level
- interests
- number of family members
- recent purchases
- where they live.

Some sites require visitors to register before they can get beyond an introductory page. The registration form is typically short and asks for general information rather than name, e-mail address and inside leg measurement – which visitors may be reluctant to give until they know you a bit better! Once the form is filled out, visitors get a confirmation and a password (sometimes by e-mail) to access the site. *Wired* magazine's web site, HotWired, was the first to go down this route in 1994. The data gathered allowed HotWired to become one of the first web sites to sell advertising. Since it was based on real information, advertisers were happy to pay to be part of it. Now it is commonplace.

It doesn't always work
Lots of web visitors dislike being tracked and will avoid sites that do so. They also provide false information (just to throw off the statistics), false e-mail addresses (so they don't get pestered) and give out their password to others. HotWired's most popular visitor ever was 'cypherpunk', but thousands of visitors knew it and used it.

To get the most accurate results keep the form short, simple and non-intrusive.

But when it does, it's wonderful
Tracking information can also have an immediate impact. If you enter a keyword in AltaVista, for instance, you will probably see a banner ad linked to your search. If you had a property-letting site and expressed an interest in houses in, say, Yorkshire, the tracking software could arrange to fill the site with links to car rental companies, visitor attractions, restaurants within a 20-mile radius. Companies will pay well if you can convince them that their information is getting to specific, targeted groups.

USING BOTH METHODS

Find a web counter or stats service which tells you what you want to know (try a few or even more than one at a time) and design your own form to collect the more detailed information on individual visitors.

Step 8

Improve Your Site

SUPERCHARGE YOUR WEB SITE

Your web site is there and it works. But could it work better? Could it have more components and functionality? Could it be more of an asset to your business? Of course it could.

DESIGN CONSIDERATIONS

A site can be as designery, colourful and attractive as you like, but if it doesn't work or doesn't do its job, it's a waste of time, web space and phone calls.

- Keep your graphics files small. The more graphics, the longer the page will take to load and the more likely it is that the visitor will hit the Stop button or go elsewhere. Balance the 'wow' and the 'now' of graphics. Even on a 56k modem (which not everyone has) a 4KB image will take one second to load. And if you have 20 graphics?
- Bigger files take longer – so your company logo may be super-duper, all-dancing animation and cost an arm and a leg from the multimedia mob downstairs, but who is going to wait a minute or more to see it? You can reduce file sizes by cutting down the number of colours – use eight instead of 16 or 256. If your graphics must have lots of colours, save them as jpg files. If not, use gif. If using gif, specify an optimised palette (which will contain only the colours actually used). Only use the resolution you need – there is little point in producing an image at 600 dpi (dots per inch) when the typical computer screen displays at 86 dpi or less.
- Use standard fonts other browsers will have loaded. Stick to the Netscape 216 colour palette.

NAVIGATION

A site that doesn't allow visitors to see what it contains and how to get there is not going to get much traffic. Worse, if the navigation is confusing or counter-intuitive, they'll get lost and just give up.

- Think of it as a road map – derive everything from the home page and provide a clear path back to it from everywhere. Clearly indicate all destinations, and at all times allow the visitors to see where they are, where they can go, and how to get back to where they came from.

- Your site's navigation is a guide – think what you would want to know and where you would want to go if you encountered the site for the first time. You may remember that the order form is in *www.mysite/folder1/folder1a/order/order2/form.htm*, but will anyone else, and why is it anyway? Try to make the physical structure of the site reflect its organisation – have different groups of pages in separate folders (images, products, orders, database, etc) with a suitably named page in the root to lead them to that folder.

- Don't be clever with names. If you have a customer contact form, call it *customer_contact.htm*, put it in a folder called *customer_contact* and make sure its title is Customer Contact Form. Likewise, call your initial page *index.htm* or *default.htm* and make its title Home or perhaps MyCompany Home.

- Point with pictures. Perhaps an image is a better way to label a navigation link than a word. If you have departments of your site dealing with shoes, staples and sandwiches, get a relevant picture or clip art image and use that as the link label.

- However, don't be too tricky – the reason a picture is worth a thousand words is that there may be a thousand ways to interpret an image without context. If you saw an image of an elephant, would you assume it was a link to a listing of zoos, or to a page about the nature of memory? Perhaps it's obvious from the site's overall theme, but it may not be. Add a text label to make it obvious. The worst offenders for this are web designers (many of them working for the EU in Brussels!) who assume that if they put up a flag, everyone will know what language that refers to. Are you clear on the difference between the Swedish, Danish and Italian flags? Exactly.

- Every graphic should have **ALT** text associated with it – and something meaningful, not just wdfr1462.gif – because:

   (a) when the mouse goes over it, the visitor gets an extra inkling as to what it's about

   (b) some perverse people always have their graphics turned off to make the page load faster, so even if your visitors have pictures turned off they can still read and use your navigation

   (c) even if the image is an elephant and the label says

elephant.htm, putting 'Click here to see a picture of an elephant' underneath is a great help to some people. Oh, you'd be surprised.

Be careful with images and image maps

- An image map is a picture which contains a number of links at different places within the image. Clicking on each **hot spot** links to a different file. This is fine and can be extremely effective – imagine a map of Europe where clicking on each country took you to the page describing the wine of that country, say. But if the graphics are turned off, it won't work. So always provide **textual hyperlinks** as well.
- There are still some potential customers out there with text-only browsers. This is why you often see text navigation (<Home> <Back> <Next> and so on) along the bottom of the page.

Navigation types

There are three basic types of navigation:

- **Hierarchical** – best for information-rich sites organised in a tree structure.
- **Global** – ideal for 'linear' sites, where you are led from one step to another (like How To Join or an on-line How To manual).
- **Mixed** – you may have a few categories of pages with a lot of depth in them, such as lists of Books, Bikes and Bee-keeping Equipment.

Hierarchical navigation

The best examples of this are directories like Yahoo *(http://www.yahoo.com.)* You take off down a trail into increasingly specialised content and the only way back from it is back along the trail (or starting again completely). But the 'trail' is laid out for you in a tree diagram so you can go back a few steps and explore another branch.

Global and mixed navigation

These work best with on sites with navigation which allows jumping between topics. But be prepared to mix navigation schemes to make your site as user-friendly and obvious as possible – and never, ever leave a visitor at the end of a long tunnel without a clear way back. They will switch off and go watch TV instead. Or worse still, buy their next widget from another site with a better structured layout.

Navigation aids

The simplest navigation is the **embedded link** – for information on cheeses, click here (with both cheeses and here linking to the same document). A good use for this is where you don't want to interrupt the flow of a paragraph by stopping to explain a concept, as in:

Our company specialises in Business Process Re-engineering with a focus on Just In Time management.

The links would take you to expanded explanations of the big words, or to a relevant page elsewhere on the site – or some other site entirely.

The most common navigation aid is the bar on the left or at the top with the main categories of the site. You've seen it a lot, because it works and everyone knows how to use it. A combination of the two can be very effective – the 'top level' along the top, under the site logo; the 'child level' (pages underneath the one being viewed) down the side and 'same level' along the bottom. Yes, that's taking up a lot of space that could have content in it, but you do want people to get around and stay with you.

Graphical tabs (like the tabs on paper file separators) are an easily understood metaphor.

Frames can be useful – the navigation sits in the left-hand frame and the content loads in the right, for example – but:

- not everyone's browser can read frames
- search engines do not index framed pages
- frames can be confusing – it is harder to print or bookmark a framed page
- anyone who happens to come across the framed page 'unframed', as it were, will have no navigation (so put text navigation in each page as well)
- your framed pages may end up framed in someone else's framed page if they linked from elsewhere, and it can all end up looking like a dog's breakfast.

I hate frames – did you guess?

If you don't mind people with older browsers or Java turned off missing the point, you could save on space, avoid complicated paths and look pretty clever by including one of the multimedia or applet-based navigation tricks, such as:

- click on a link and the next page opens in a small JavaScript pop-up window
- put the mouse over a navigation element and it expands to show more detail below it

- include a site mapper with an organisation chart of your site and a complete listing of pages.

This can be cute and even useful, but they also take longer to download than text or a small image, and won't work on all browsers.

Automatic navigation generation

If your site is designed with FrontPage, NetObjects Fusion or certain other web creation tools, much of the hard work of navigation is done for you. After you choose the general navigation scheme and the overall structure of your site, the program will create the navigation bars or whatever. They can be changed easily so you can try different options and combinations.

WEB DATABASES

One way to make your web site attractive to visitors is to provide information they would otherwise find it hard or inconvenient to get themselves. Another way is to make it interactive. A third way is to keep it fresh with new, relevant information. You can combine all three by operating a web database.

Say you sell model railways. It is likely that the visitors to your site would be interested in a list of upcoming events and exhibitions, or information on the latest offerings from model train manufacturers, or even just a list of e-mail addresses and phone numbers of modelling clubs. This is a database you would probably find useful yourself and may even have. If not, why not? Running an e-business means getting as much information as possible into computerised form and using it to its best advantage.

It is equally likely that if you had such a database and others found it useful, it would drive visitors to your site. This is the thinking behind the Local Hotel Web databases run by Tourist Boards and the AA and also the whole concept behind Amazon.com.

If your business is actually database-driven – like an advertising magazine, an estate agent or an insurance broker – then give users access to it via the web. Exchange and Mart (*http://www.exchange andmart.co.uk/*) is one big database, updated every time someone phones or sends in an advertisement. Another good example is Booksearch UK (*http://www.booksearchuk.co.uk/*).

Getting your database on-line

This is complicated, but not quite the black art it is often made out to be. However, it is not as straightforward as simple web page design.

If you are a large company with an in-house server, you probably have the expertise to do it. Your IT people will talk you into a ColdFusion-enabled or Oracle-based system, and good for them.

If you are a very small business with your site hosted elsewhere, it can be frustrating to say the least. You will need either a **CGI (common gateway interface)** script to search the database or you will need to construct your site using FrontPage, which has basic but robust data handling tools. Neither is a job for an amateur.

CGI scripts

A CGI script is an executable program, usually written in language like Perl. First, check whether your ISP or WSP allows CGI scripts to be run – many do not. Then check whether they have a library of CGI scripts available, including a database search script. If so, get as much detail as you can on how it works and what you need to do. Even if you do not write your own CGI scripts, you will have to put the 'queries' (the commands which tell the script which database to search and for what) into your web pages. There are on-line script archives and tutorials and Matt's Script Archive (*http://scriptarchive.com/* and *http://www.cgi-resources.com/*) is as good a starting point as any.

FrontPage

Microsoft's web page design tool is fast becoming a favourite for constructing sites and it uses a variant of ASP (active server page) technology to provide database access without CGI programming. An associated product, VisualStudio, has a range of development tools to help further. To run a FrontPage web, your server must have FrontPage extensions installed. These are additional files which make FrontPage webs rattle and hum. Not all ISPs operate FrontPage servers and those that do may charge extra. If you go down this route, take the opportunity to use FrontPage to its fullest extent and get a jazzed-up web site out of it. FrontPage 98 was available free for a while but is now hard to find since FrontPage 2000 was launched. There is a 45-day demo version of this available from Microsoft (*http://www.microsoft.co.uk/*) for the cost of the postage.

FrontPage Express

Microsoft's simple (and free) web page design tool has the capability to build in a **search form**, which searches for text in your site. This can be used to provide access to other pages (see below). FP Express should have come with your Internet Explorer. If not, upgrade to IE5 or download FP Express separately from Microsoft. It is widely available on PC magazine CDs.

Keep it simple

If all you want to do is provide information on 30 upcoming events, 40 suppliers' addresses or a catalogue of 50 items, it may be simpler to have these as 30, 40 or 50 individual web pages accessible from hyperlinks in a web page made to look like a database. You will have to change the information pages and the text in the links as the data change, which can be time-consuming.

Alternatively, use FrontPage Express to create a page containing a **webbot** (a piece of built-in programming) which searches for text in web pages. Put all your informational pages in a new folder and direct the form to search in that folder only instead of 'All'.

WEB TELEPHONES

The internet uses the phone lines to send data to and from anywhere in the world, for the price of a local phone call. So why not use it for phone calls to anywhere in the world? This drive telecomms providers crazy since they can't charge high call rates. If carried to extremes, it will completely clog international phone lines. In the meantime, it's a great way to keep in touch with home and office from abroad.

If your computer has a sound card, speakers and a microphone, all you need is some specialised software to make internet phone calls. If you have Netscape Navigator 3 or above, you may have the appropriate software. Some modems also bundle it with their installation programs. Mine (which was not expensive – around £50) came with WebPhone and Net2Phone, which are slightly different.

WebPhone

Features include:

- point-to-point voice and video over the internet or any TCP/IP-based network
- real-time full-duplex voice communications
- integrated voice mail system
- call holding, muting, do not disturb and caller ID
- speed dial, redial and call conferencing
- video phone support using International Standard H.263
- state-of-the-art cellular phone interface for ease-of-use.

WebPhone costs $49.95 (£31) or $19.95 (£12.50) for the Home version.

Net2Phone (*http://www.net2phone.com/*)

This is not strictly speaking an internet phone program, but a way of connecting to a cheap international call rate service which places calls for you and charges your credit card for the time (you have to register). It has the advantage that you can place calls to a standard phone anywhere. At the time of writing the call rate from the UK to America was 10–15c (7–10p) per minute. Net2Phone also provides free access to US toll free (800) and (888) numbers from anywhere else. However, it cannot operate from behind a firewall, so may not be an ideal solution for a company with its own server. There are ways around this – consult *http://www.net2phone.com/english/ts.html* for ideas.

There is also a facility called Click2Talk (*http://www.click2talk.com/*) which enables customers to speak to your staff by clicking a button in your web site.

Firetalk (*http://destinationsite.com/*)

This online communication software combines voice and text communication. Features include:

- free conference calling to up to 100 other Firetalk users
- free group web tours – link browsers and surf together while talking
- free voice chatrooms for web sites – hold a voice chat session on any web site on the internet including your own
- free voice mail and instant messaging – leave voice or text messages for other Firetalk users
- free worldwide calls, but only to other Firetalk users.

Hardware hints

- Check that your sound card is SoundBlaster compatible – it's the commonest standard.
- Like a telephone, a **full-duplex soundcard** enables you to talk and listen at the same time.
- Invest in a headset (earphones and microphone) to improve quality and leave both hands free. A halfway decent one costs less than £15. More than that buys better quality.

TOP TIPS

If you build it, will they come? No. Having a web site is not an end in itself. The champagne popped at the party when you go on-line for the first time will go a bit flat when you've had 34 visitors after six months. The hard work starts once a site goes on-line, so promote, refine and improve it constantly.

1 Be consistent most of the time

Fine – you're getting lots of hits on your site, your e-mail in-tray is full of replies and filled-in forms and you have a hundred links out there on other pages. But consider – are all the hits and e-mails generating sales? If not, which ones are and why? Consider this, then reshape your site or your e-mail campaign to generate more responses from those that convert to sales. One customer from ten hits is better than no customers from a thousand.

2 Be involved

Personal involvement will enhance your understanding of what the internet is and can do for you. So answer e-mails, take part in on-line mailing lists and newsgroup discussions, become recognised as an interested, authoritative figure in your community of interest. Include your site in a **web ring**.

3 Be ready for the unforeseen

You'll never get your print catalogue to Sweden, but they may see your web site. Are you ready for this? Likewise you may never have thought about selling to government departments, schools or hospitals but their on-line procurement search may turn you up as a prospect. Can you handle it?

4 Clients can link too

If your clients have web sites, put a 'Client Links' page in with company names, short descriptions, e-mail address and a link to their URL. This builds existing customer loyalty, prospective customer trust and your reputation as an established e-business. But do ask them first, and also ask for a reciprocal link on their site. Use e-mail testimonials too – the 'third-party sell' works on-line.

5 FAQs

If you have a page of the most frequently asked questions from customers and prospective customers, and the answers, you are not only providing a valuable service, you are cutting down the number of enquiry phone calls or e-mails you will have to answer.

6 Form follows function, function follow needs

Your web site isn't really about you – it's about them, the customers.
So give them the information and services they need. Believe me,
they don't care about values statements, company philosophies, mis-
sions, visions, strategies, objectives and organisational growth charts.
Your aim is to shorten the sales cycle length and reduce business friction, not recycle your MBA notes.

7 Keep an eye on it

Check your progress, not just to see how your site is doing, but also
to keep you motivated or give you the shot in the arm you need if
you aren't. Every month or so search for your company name in one
of the large search engines. The number of search results returned
indicates the number of other sites linked to you, which will tell you
how well exposed and well recognised you are. Look at those pages
(they will most likely be of relevance to your business) for new ideas
on style, presentation, tricks etc.

Always look out for ways to make your web site better – whether
it's a new design element or better technology such as a shopping
cart or database management facility or just a way to make it faster.
The more automated your site, the longer you can spend on the golf
course, talking to your family or inventing new business rather than
answering e-mails.

9 Links, recht, links, recht

I'll show you mine if you show me yours, so let's link to each other.
Find sites that interest your typical target customer (by thinking like
them) and offer reciprocal linking. This is a time-consuming job and
best done in the dead of night when phone calls are cheap and the
web a bit quicker. Do a few each day, possibly while you're downloading something else – you may as well use the bandwidth.

10 Patience man, patience

Your web marketing plan ought to be one line long – 'I will grow the
exposure of my web site and sales will follow'. But it will take six
months before you see much difference. Don't lose heart.

11 Promote your URL

Is your web address and e-mail on all of your printed material – business cards, letterheads, fliers, catalogues and price lists, fax cover
sheet, invoices, purchase orders, answerphone message, shop sign,
company car? Why not? It is even better if you have a domain name

related to your company name or business type (*we-are-shoes.com* or *fishing.net*). And is your URL on your products? Not just the packaging but the product itself? If you make shoes, does the sole have the URL moulded in backwards so it leaves a right-way-round imprint in every muddy puddle? Now there's free advertising for you. A client of mine has a number of web sites, all for different purposes and all of which look different. And extremely artistic they are, too. So he had them reproduced on postcards which he uses as mailshots, known collectively as 'Postcards from the Edge'.

12 Use the search engines – everyone else does

This is the most important way of people finding your site. See page 79 for details about meta tags and search engine listing, and check each major search engine, directory and portal every month for your ranking and listing. If you add a new page, resubmit your site to the search engines. When the search engines bring up sites that aren't yours, look at these. View them in Internet Explorer, use the View Source toolbar command and mercilessly steal their meta tag keywords, descriptions etc.

Set some simple and about all attainable goals at the outset and revise these constantly just as you would with any business plan. Examples might be:

- Add 100 new prospects to my mailing list per month.
- Cut promotional costs by 50% by using the web.
- Have ten new clients in the next year.
- Increase sales by ten per cent through web marketing this year.

14 What's so special about you, then?

What's your **unique selling point** (**USP**)? Don't waste time telling the world why you're the same as everyone else – tell them what distinctive difference your company, product or service has. On the web everybody can be different. So go be different.

15 Why they buy on the web – or not

Why do they buy? It saves time. Why don't they buy? They can't look at or try out the product first. If your product is software, you can issue a free demo. If it's information, give a taster or a sample chapter free. If it's more tangible than that, turn a good photo into a **jpeg file** (linked from a smaller, low-quality and fast-loading gif image). If you believe in your product, give a 100% money-back guarantee. If other customers have linked it and said so, include testimonials (after asking permission and sending the customer a small thank-you present).

16 You are a professional, but does your web site say so?

If your web site isn't taken seriously, you won't be either. If you can't afford a tip-top designer or don't have those skills, get one of the professionally designed templates that are out there on the web or come with the web building packages.

17 Get your own domain name

You won't make an impression if your site is obviously part of some free hosting service. The first impression of something like *www.some-freedeal.co.uk/handyparts/* is nowhere near as impressive and confidence-inspiring as *www.handyparts.co.uk*. The image you portray is someone who isn't making enough money to spend £20 a year on domain registration.

18 Give away free information

Which local businesses do you like best? The ones who will give you help, advice, guidance and free information. You are likely to go back to a garage, hardware shop or electrical store which will take the time to help you with technical queries. The same is true of a web site. People don't buy from web sites or shops – they buy from other people they trust.

19 Does your site look professional?

Designing a web site is easy. But if it looks like it was knocked up with a box of kids' crayons it won't impress anyone. Ask a few people who have an axe to grind for their honest opinions of your site – in terms of design and functionality – and take their comments seriously.

20 Is the text effective?

The words on your site should be concise, accurate, free of spelling and grammatical howlers and professional. The intention is to motivate visitors to do something.

21 Do you have a privacy/security statement?

Let your visitors know what you will do – and won't do – with any information they send. It inspires confidence to know that you won't share e-mail addresses or ordering information with anyone else. Or if you intend to do that, say so and ask them to agree or disagree. TRUSTe (*http://www.etrust.com/wizard/*) has a wizard to construct a statement for you.

22 Is your credit card ordering secure?
If it is, say so. Get a merchant account with a **secure order form**.

23 Sell one thing – well
A web site with hundreds of products and services is hard to maintain. Concentrate on a small number of good products and sell them consistently. Don't try to sell them everything at the first visit – humans do not buy things if they are confused or pressured.

24 Develop an e-mail list
If you want your visitors to give you their e-mail addresses, offer a free e-newsletter, discounts, news, hints and tips or something else genuinely free and valuable. Use a simple sign-up form – if you ask a hundred questions they will get bored and go away, or worry that you are being intrusive. You don't want to scare them off.

25 Contact your e-mail list regularly
Publish a weekly e-mail newsletter, a monthly hints page and quarterly special offers. It costs a lot less time, effort and money to get a return visitor than to generate a new one. Your best future sales prospects are your past customers!

26 Promote your website regularly and well
If your site sells something to every 1,000th visitor and you get 1,000 visitors a week, the chances are you will double your sales if you get 2,000 visitors. Step 10 (page 111) deals with this in more detail.

Step 9

Start Selling Online

ADVANTAGES OF AN ON-LINE SHOP

Even as recently as early 1999 **on-line shopping, shopping baskets** and **database-driven catalogue sites** were at the cutting edge of web technology and were expensive to construct, hard to manage and a specialist job to maintain. Now everything is simpler – more user-friendly shop creation programs, improved transaction handling and the huge demand for e-commerce have brought this within the reach of almost anyone. You really can have an on-line shop up and ready to take orders within days or even hours.

At its best, a web-based selling mechanism has a lot of things going for it:

- open 24 hours a day
- no staff costs, rent, utility bills or other overheads, other than your time and your phone bills
- no stock requirement (if you are not selling physical goods which you have to warehouse)
- good cash flow (you get the money first and can re-stock, if you have to, from payments in)
- customers can be tracked – you have their e-mails and credit card details
- global reach.

THE ON-LINE SHOP

The basic components of an on-line shop are:

- a web site showing or describing your products or services
- a payment system
- one or more databases for stock details, customer details and orders

Things to consider when setting up a catalogue and payment system include:

- Do you need multiple catalogue pages? If you are selling, say, a wide range of jewellery or books or specialist food items or electronic components, your catalogue might be quite extensive.
- Do you need different 'departments'? If you are selling hand-made teddy bears, four kinds of home-made honey and CDs, you may want these in different catalogues sections.
- What price are your goods or services? The charges associated with on-line credit card transactions may make small payments uneconomical. Would you expect to take a Visa card for a 50p bag of sweets in a shop? Likewise, retain credit card sales for items costing over, say £110. There are micropayment systems available for smaller sums (see below).
- Do you want to offer a cheque payment facility? If someone wishes to pay by cheque, have a page which can be printed out as an order form to send along with payment. Consider setting up a FREEPOST address to make it painless for them (ask your local Post Office for details) but add the cost to the post and packing charge.
- Will you be taking orders from abroad? You need to consider foreign currency transactions without getting stuck with a massive handling or conversion charge. And make sure you can accept payments in Euros.
- On the other hand, credit card payments from abroad aren't so much a problem since they get translated automatically from and to the appropriate currencies – you don't worry about using your UK card to buy in dollars from a shop in Spain, do you? Not for that reason, anyway!
- Will there be multiple choices? It is a complete pain for a customer to have to leave and re-enter your on-line shop to choose more than one item. Don't get caught in this trap.
- How will you price the post and packing? It is only fair that customers know the price up front (and you have to charge for it on-line) so it has to be determined. Options are to charge by weight or per unit. If you are selling things which weigh the same, you can add a per-item cost which is known. If they vary in weight, the shipping costs will have to be determined separately. Some e-commerce programs allow both options, but it depends on knowing the weights of everything. You can also offer a choice of mailing methods – first and second class, surface or airmail, parcel post or courier. Any decent e-commerce package will have these options built in, but you have to enter the costs.
- VAT is an issue. Do you know which of your goods attract VAT and at which rate? Find out before you sell them. Even if you are

not registered for VAT you still have to charge it.

- Do you actually have to carry stock? If you are selling, say, Scottish produce from a range of producers, do a deal with them which means you receive the initial order and eventual payment and send them the orders to fulfil – they do the packing and postage. You have to be able to trust them, because dissatisfied customers are going to come back to you (as the merchant) not the suppliers.
- Can you offer other products alongside your own? If you sell pot plants, establish a link with Amazon so that customers can get gardening books. You will receive a small commission and will never have to pack and post the books. Money for nothing! There are any number of 'reseller' options, link exchanges and banner deals which will net you trouble-free extra income. These are dealt with in more detail later (see page111).

YOUR ELECTRONIC TILL

All of the above assumed that you would be taking credit card payments by some mechanism. There are three basic ways to organise this.

1 If you are already a merchant (ie can take physical credit cards) your card company or bank may allow you to set up an on-line transaction system.
2 If you don't have that facility, or don't want it, there are payment companies which will do it for you. NetBanx is one example. This may well be an included option if you buy an e-commerce solution such as ShopFactory or Shop@ssistant.
3 If you are reselling someone else's goods (such as books via Amazon or CDs via CDNow) they will handle all payments and send you any commission on a quarterly basis.

SECURE TRANSACTIONS

If you want to organise your own credit card transactions, you will need a secure web site. Even if someone else is processing transactions for you, it may still be a good idea – especially if people are sending you secure information by e-mail after filling in forms.

A normal web site sends images, text, any formatting associated with text (HTML) and any other components you may have added (dynamic HTML, Java applets etc) over the internet in plain text. This is reinterpreted by the user's browser into the page as designed. But this is insecure – anyone who could intercept it could read it. And since it may pass through hundreds of computers on its way from the server to the browser, the possibilities are high.

It was this which prevented many people from sending any kind of sensitive, personal or financial information by internet for a long time, and the reason why dedicated networks (like those owned by the banks) were necessary. However, there are now secure web sites. This depends on an **encryption** process understood only by the server and the receiving browser. Any information transferred is encrypted (coded) and, even if intercepted, cannot be read as anything meaningful. Suddenly, sending your credit card number was more secure than if you had handed it over in a restaurant.

ENCRYPTION SCHEMES

The commonest encryption technologies are Secure Sockets Layer (SSL) and Secure HTTP (S-HTTP), plus a standard from e-mail called PGP.

How encryption works

Imagine you wanted to pass on a secret number to a friend, and you agreed that you would post him the number, but that you would multiply it (and he would divide it) by 12. So if you want to send the number '8', you send 96 and your partner knows to divide it to get 8 again. That's fine even if someone intercepts your letter, because they could not work out from the 96 that the 'key' is 12. But it would be possible, given enough messages, to work out what the encryption key must be. However, suppose you agreed to multiply and divide it using a key that changed each time. You agree to transform the 'message' number using the 'private' key (12) plus a number which changes each time, but which you will also send each time. Your letter contains the message (136) and the 'public' key (say 5). Your partner knows to divide this by 12+5 = 17 to get 8, but anyone who intercepts the letter doesn't know what the 5 is combined with or whether it is added, subtracted, multiplied or whatever. It would take far more message intercepts to work it out and what's more, it changes each time. Imagine how much more secure this becomes when the two keys are hundreds of numbers long. It would take a great deal of computing power to crack it, even if there were enough time to do so.

This is the basis of a number of encryption routines. One called PGP (Pretty Good Privacy) is so good that it was almost banned by the US government (who feel they have an interest in being able to read anyone's e-mails) and the inventor was harassed, given the full

FBI treatment and almost prosecuted as a traitor for exposing state secrets. It became a *cause célèbre* in the civil liberties and free-speech movements.

At the time of writing, non-US programs could use 40-bit encryption (keys using 2^{40} or about 1 trillion characters) and the highest level available was 128-bit (you work it out).

SSL

This was developed by Netscape and is a part of almost all web servers. Both Netscape and Internet Explorer browsers can handle it, as can others. You can tell that you are in a secure site because the URL may start with *https://* instead of the normal *http://* and in the bottom of your browser window there will be a small padlock or a key which will either be open (indicating a non-secure server) or closed (a secure server). If you would like to see examples of this, go to a known secure site such as *http://www.amazon.co.uk/* and choose a book. Proceed with the ordering and checkout details as far as you need to get to the secure site. You don't have to actually order anything. Double-clicking on the padlock brings up a window with security information, including the **site certificate** (see below and Figure 3).

If you plan to operate a commercial business via the internet, check that your ISP supports SSL. It may be free, or available as an additional service at extra cost. Your server needs to have a **digital certificate** which is used by the encryption program to generate a public key and to authenticate the server. This is certified by one of the many Certification Authorities of which Verisign (*http://www.verisign.com/*) is the best known. Another place to start is *http://www.microsoft.com/windows/oe/certpage.asp* (see below for e-mail information). If you are doing this yourself, check your web server's documentation for the particular steps to take and which SSL software to use.

S-HTTP

This is very similar to SSL and is free (available from *http://www.nsca.org/*) but is not so widely supported as the proprietary SSL. Both Netscape and Internet Explorer will support it soon and both browsers will be able to connect to S-HTTP or SSL servers.

Encryption for e-mail

Most modern e-mail programs can send and receive encrypted e-mail, sometimes after acquiring a **plug-in** or additional software module. Check your e-mail software's help file or documentation. For

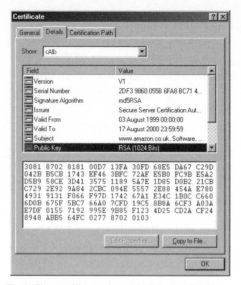

Fig. 3. Site certificate viewed in Internet Explorer.

example, Outlook Express can be set up to include a digital ID certificate (a combination of a public key and a 'digital signature'). Recipients use your digital signature to verify who you are and use your public key to send encrypted mail only you can read (using your private key). To send encrypted messages, your Address Book must have the digital IDs of the recipients so you can use their public keys. First, obtain a digital ID from a certification authority and set up your mail account to use it. Set this up using tools, options, security from where you can connect to a site (*http://www.microsoft.com/windows/oe/certpage.asp*) that lists Certification Authorities.

There is another security issue – protecting your web site files from download except to registered callers or after payment. This is dealt with on page 124.

CREDIT CARDS

Payment has always been the big issue for the internet. You could have the world's greatest site, millions of visitors and a superlative service or product that everyone wants – but how do you take the money? Previous solutions ('Complete this page, print it out and send it with a cheque to . . .' or 'Call this number with your credit card details . . .') have proved less than satisfactory. They're in your site *now* and you want them to purchase *now*. Any delays or extra processes and the impulse may go away. Imagine a high street shop saying: 'Yes, we have shirts in stock of your size. Please send us a cheque and when it clears, come back and collect your purchase.' This is another example of **friction** in transactions.

Taking credit card details over the internet is relatively easy. It was solved largely by 'adult' video and web site producers who wanted a trusted and reliable way of getting hold of your cash instantly. The only thing that prevented its widescale adoption was concerns over security, but these have largely been solved (see above). The issue is not really one of individual fraud or risk – why, and indeed how, would some electronic eavesdropper pick on your £19.99 book purchase out of the thousands of electronic messages sent every second? It is about confidence – no major retailer would trust the system enough to ask customers to trust it.

Out of this came secure payment systems, based on encryption algorithms and secure sites. The commonest form of electronic cash transfer is by using a normal credit card and sending the details (card type and number, expiry date, cardholder's name) to a secure site, often one managed by a bank. The full information may never actually reach the retailer, further ensuring your protection from internet fraud – all they get are the last four digits of your card number. The commonest set-up for this is SSL (see above). Other solutions include:

- Virtual debit card – you run an account with a bank which is debited each time you make a purchase from a secure site.
- Virtual bank note (or token) – you buy credit from an internet bank, who bill you, your credit card or your 'real' bank account monthly by normal mechanisms such as cheques or direct debit.
- Intermediary banking – a variation on one of the above, but the seller never knows who you are, only that you have paid.
- Response billing – you provide a phone or fax number by which the retailer contacts the buyer to ask for credit card details.
- Secure e-mail – an encrypted message is sent along with e-mail, including credit card details.

Variations on these have been adopted by different providers.
So the technology exists to:

- Ensure that credit card details are not readable by anyone except the legitimate recipient (SSL and digital certificates).
- Give comfort to the customer that the retailer will not be able to re-use the card details (trusted third party involvement, such as a bank).
- Assure the retailer that payment will be made.

There is one piece missing from that puzzle, however: what guarantee is there that the user really is the cardholder? The chances of a stolen credit card being used for internet purchases is far, far higher than that of a real transaction being fraudulently misapplied. To solve this, MasterCard and Visa have set up a new system called SET (Secure Electronic Transactions). More information is available at the two relevant sites: (*http://www.mastercard.com/* and *http://www.visa.com/*).

So how do you set yourself up for credit card payments over the internet?

JOIN AN E-MALL

Just as a shopping mall developer will rent you shop space and look after things like cleaning, lighting and security, an **e-mall** owner will provide you with web space, a shop front and all the 'back-office' functions. The first major example of this was Barclay Square (*http://www.barclaysquare.co.uk/*) and many others have followed suit.

Pros
- Little or no hassle to set up the site
- May be exclusive in whom they allow to join
- May be specific to one locality or business sector
- Few hidden costs
- Handle all transactions
- Lots of publicity, exposure visitors.

Cons
- Little control over site look, feel and design
- May be *too* exclusive in whom they allow to join
- May be *too* specific, or not specific enough
- Can be expensive
- May not pay promptly
- But they may not come to your shop, and you can't change that.

SITE SHOPS AND TURNKEY SOLUTIONS

This is a slightly different idea along the same lines – a company provides you with a web template (so you don't have to do any design) and all the transactional, site submission and visitor tracking tools, then hosts your site for you. Very basic examples are Netscape's service (*http://smallbusiness.netscape.com/smallbusiness/main.tmpl*), Amazon's z-Shops (*http://www.amazon.co.uk*) and shop-yahoo (*http://shop.yahoo.com/*). There are more controllable systems, in the sense that you have some hand in the design and you appear to be operating an 'independent' site. IBM's HomePage Creator (*http://www.ibm.com/businesscentre/uk/*) is a well-known example as is Electrom (*http://www.electrom.com/*) which is specialised for Front-Page users (see pages 90–2).

Pros	Cons
• Easy to set up the site	• All sites tend to look the same
• May allow you to design a site 'off' their standard templates and upload it to join	• May not allow certain prosite programming techniques (frames, CGI etc)
• Single monthly or annual charge	• Often, a confusing set of payment options
• Low 'basic' cost	• But try doing anything even slightly demanding and watch the charges spiral
• Handle all transactions	• May not pay promptly
• You can control and dictate visitor targeting and tracking.	• It may get very lonely if no one comes.

RESELLER LINKS

If all you wanted to do was sell books, CDs or other products related to your business or interest, you can become an Affiliate, Associate or Reseller (the terms vary) of mother's products. For instance, you can buy this book via a link from my site straight to Amazon who will do everything including posting you the book and send me a percentage as a commission. In fact, I make more from a sale that way than from the ensuing royalty payment! Likewise you could sell other people's software, hardware and information and you take no part in the process other than collecting the commission cheques. This method can be additional to any individual payment system you set up for yourself.

THIRD PARTY BANKING

All transactions are handled by an intermediary, who may charge you a commission per sale or a standard charge per transaction, per month or per year. An example of the first is NetBanx (*http://www.netbanx.com/*) who will process all transactions and send you the income less any charges. IBM's HomePage Creator and Electrom (see above) are examples of site hosts who also provide transaction processing as part of the standard charge. Those who use FrontPage to design sites can get an add-on called JustAdd Commerce (*http://www.richmediatech.com*) which adds back-office processing to a self-designed site. Most stand-alone shop creation programs have a similar facility. In both cases the site can be hosted anywhere and the product details, ordering forms etc are part of that, but the actual ordering and payment take place on the software company's secure server.

Be aware that you may be offered a choice of a standard charge per month, a charge per item or a percentage of the individual or total transaction values. You will have to calculate which is the better deal for you, but bear in mind:

- There may be a minimum regardless of the number of sales (even if none).
- You can rest assured that if you are bringing in £1 million a month and paying the standard £19.99, the company concerned will soon shift you to the percentage-of-value model.
- Check how and when you can cancel the arrangement – try not to get locked in for a year or have to pay a high penalty to cancel.

MERCHANT SERVICES

If you already accept credit cards (as many 'real' shops do) you have what is called a **merchant account**. You can extend this to an on-line merchant account. Either ask your existing bank or card service provider for details, or use one of the reliable third parties (NetBanx, VeriSign, most of the others listed above or even your own ISP).

It will be a matter for your own judgement which of these options is the best for you, but bear in mind you have to add up the costs in Figure 4 (page 109). I have used real examples with prices correct at the time of writing and all charges are the annual totals, although they may in practice by payable monthly.

	IBM HomePage Creator	Electrom	DIY with ShopFactory
• ISP annual dial-up cost	£0 - £240	£0-240	£0-£240
• WSP annual hosting fee	£240-£1500	Free, or £240-£400	Up to £200
• Annual domain name registration fee	£0 for alias*, otherwise from £5	£0 for alias*, otherwise from £5	From £5
• Annual e-commerce charges (secure server, NetBanx etc)	About £300 (NetBanx)	May be free	About £300 (NetBanx) but could take card numbers manually (free)
• Purchase cart etc	£0	£0 (but extra charges for additional functions	£200 - £500 depending on version

*'Alias' means here, you get a subsite of the provider's site. For instance, I have set one up for this book at *http://www23.electrom.com/ebusinessessential/index.htm* but I could pay to have it aliased to *http://www.e-business-essentials.com* (a 'real' site).

For more comparisons of e-commerce shop creation programs, consult *http://www.site-omatic.co.uk/Warning/Comparison2/comparison2.htm* and *http://www.wilsonweb.com/cgibin/ubb/Ultimate.cgi/* not wholly unbiased in either case.

It is possible to avoid transaction processing and have credit card details sent to you by secure e-mail. You then complete card slips by hand. This is a good option for a low number of transactions. When it starts to get onerous, it is time to pay a Merchant Services company like NetBanx or CyberCash.

Fig. 4. Costs of e-commerce.

Producing web sites using a shop creation program may be the answer. In general the best advice is as set out in the table on page 110.

	Small number of transactions	**Large number of transactions**
Small number of items	Sign up with *shop.yahoo.com. zShops* etc	Design your own site using a shop creation program and host it with your WSP under your own domain name. Invest in Merchant software to handle your own order processing (or use your ISP's) but don't pay a charge-per-item or percentage.
Large number of items	Why are you bothering? Unless each transaction is for a reasonable amount, of course (like selling computers, cars, yachts, houses or expensive software), in which case use a third-party Merchant Service which charges per month, not a percentage of each transaction or the total.	You are really in business! Negotiate with your ISP to set up a secure site with shopping cart, payment system, own merchant account, etc and have a professional site make-over by a big design company. Then sell it and retire to Barbados before the e-bubble bursts.

Step 10

Finding New Customers

Your new, improved web site is up and running, you have something to sell, you have refined your site and your processes, you know who is visiting and whether or not (and what) they buy and you have a number of subscribers to your free e-mail newsletter. What you need now is an expanded and expanding customer base.

YOUR BEST NEW CUSTOMERS ARE YOUR BEST EXISTING CUSTOMERS

It is conventional wisdom in the high street retail trade that it costs ten times more to attract a new customer than to keep an existing one. So don't ignore the ones who have bought from you in the past. You should aim for at least 30% of your traffic to be from return visitors.

How to build loyalty and return visits

1   Reward loyalty – give discounts for repeat purchases or simply send a 'thank you' e-mail after three, five or ten responses from the same customer.
2   Build a sense of belonging to a community. If a visitor relates to your site and feels part of a community of interest, that visitor will come back often. A discussion forum or bulletin board gives an interactive feel and encourages returns.
3   You might consider adding a chat room. This is only a good idea in high-traffic sites, as an empty chat room gives a bad image and discourages returns. Try advertising specific times when you, at least, will be there (6–8 pm three nights a week, for instance). You could be on-line to your chat room at the same times as you are uploading or downloading or submitting your URL to new search.
4   Hold a weekly or monthly contest. For instance: if your site is about fishing tackle, offer a prize for a picture of the biggest, best, most odd-looking fish, post them in a new folder on your site (with thumbnails linking to larger images) and ask other visitors to vote for the best one. Then send a small but meaningful prize (a new

fishing fly, for example). If your site deals with engineering products, give a prize for the best engineering jokes – 'Q. How many engineers does it take to change a light bulb? A. You'd be better off rewiring the building and putting in floodlights.' If you have a favourite freeware or shareware (and if you are sure it can be distributed) compile it onto a CD you burn yourself and send it to competition winners. It's not much (and it doesn't cost much) but it's the thought that counts. Alternatively, buy in those CD software collections which cost around £10 and use them as prizes.

5 Make your pages fresh and update them frequently. A 'what's new' page makes the site look lively.

6 Don't add a counter until your site is a success. Or if you must yet, start it at a randomly-chosen high but not boastful number like 13,254. No one believes them anyway, but 'You are visitor number 0003' is a turn-off, especially if they come back a month later and see 'You are visitor number 0004'.

7 Your newsletter or mailing list should contain as many free offerings as possible. Use a free-mailing list service (page 134) to manage it for you.

8 Ask your visitors to put a link in their web site to yours. You should have a special 'link to this site' page with images, logos etc – and the required hyperlinks – that other web site managers can add to their pages. Make it as easy as possible for them. You can check who is linked with almost any search engine – just type **link:mysite.co.uk** in the Search box to see which sites link to yours.

9 Trade links with other web sites which have related services, content or products. Make sure that any sites you trade links with are sending you a similar amount of traffic. There are many programs which can track click-throughs from text links.

10 Think about the sites you visit most often, and why. Be open to new ideas. Trial and error (and judicious swiping of other people's good ideas, without breaking copyright laws) is the best way to find new methods and strategies.

BANNER EXCHANGES

A **banner exchange** is an agreement between you and other web site owners to swap logos and adverts. People in your site see their ads; people in their sites see yours. Sounds like a traffic idea, but a beast to manage – are you really going to contact, say 1,000 other site owners and try to talk them into it? Fortunately, you don't have to – there are **link exchange providers** who will give you a few lines of HTML to put in a web page of your choice which will display a banner ad every time that page is loaded. In return, you get your banner displayed on other sites, usually one site for every two you carry. The great trick is, the banner ads change every time your page is browsed and it's all automated for you.

There are two main types of exchange deals:

1 **Display ratio** – the number of times your banner is displayed elsewhere is based on the number of times you display someone's else's. The more visitors to your site, the more banners are seen, so the more often yours is displayed elsewhere. LinkExchange (*http://www.linkexchange.com*), the largest and best respected example, uses this methodology.

2 **Click-through ratio** – you are 'guaranteed' one visitor to your site for every two clicks on the banner ads displayed on your pages. This is very typical in 'adult' sites, where banners are often accompanied by a pleading message like 'Please please please visit my Sponsors'. I'm told. TrafficX (*http://www.TrafficX.com*) operates this way and the name says it all.

Most banner exchange programs send you detailed accounts – click-through rates, how many times banners get displayed, on what sites, at what times etc. This can help you measure and take account of the traffic to your site.

Some hints

- Be careful which page you direct people to from the ad you supply – is your start page the most appropriate one? If you sell shoes and home made jam, you should consider two exchange programs, each one category-matched and leading to the appropriate page on your site.
- Choose a program which allows category choice – you determine that your ad goes on relevant, related sites (and that the ads you get are similarly relevant).
- If the banners are too large they will take an age to load and no one will wait around to see the rest of your beautiful page. They can also look garish and unsubtle. Which you aren't, no no no.
- If you host a banner exchange on the first page of your site, then the visitor has left. Two visitors have to do that before you get one banner on someone else's site.
- Include your URL and e-mail in the banner ad. Even those who don't click may remember it for later.
- Look at banners you find attractive and ask yourself why.

- Monitor the number of click-throughs.
- On the other hand, do you want to be advertising your competitors?
- On the other hand, don't you want your competitors to be advertising you? Generally, the best place to have a shoe shop is next to another shoe shop.
- Try different designs and different programs and compare.
- Use the banner ad to give away a free gift – it could be a sample, a chance to win a free product or some information.
- You can either only host banners on the 'deeper' pages of your site (say, on the confirmation page after they've bought something) or you can send the banner link to a new window, so your site doesn't close.
- Spend a very great deal of money putting your banner ad on Netscape Netcentre, AltaVista or Yahoo! Or don't.

EXCHANGE PROGRAMS

Hyperbanner Network (*http://www.hyperbanner.net*) is similar to LinkExchange but without the category selection feature and with even bigger banners (468 × 60). However, it can be made country specific, and is there any point in you advertising in the States? It does mean that you could target certain countries – with a language specific page, say.

Info-Links Index (send a blank e-mail to *adinfo@info-links.com*) – not an exchange program as such, you pay about $10 (£7) per 1,000 'impressions'.

LinkExchange (*http://www.linkexchange.com*) is the best known but the banners are rather big (440 × 40) and must be at the top. Category selection is possible.

TrafficX (*http://www.TrafficX.com/*) 'guarantees' one visitor per two people who click on banners you display and ten guarantees for every person you introduce to their program. They have full-sized banners (400 × 40, 468 × 60) and microbanners (88 × 31) and you can place them almost anywhere.

DESIGN AN EFFECTIVE BANNER AD

This is an art in itself.

1 People like colour and movement. Bright colours attract the eye. Contrast a bright background with dark text or pictures, or vice versa. Remember that you have no control over the background

colour of the page they end up on.

2 Animated ads increase click-through rates – fact! You can also get across more information this way. But try to keep the file size to 8K.

3 Add a 'Click here' instruction – yes, most people really are that dim.

4 Good packages for constructing graphics and animations of all types are Paintshop Pro (*http://www.jasc.com/*) and GIF Construction Set (*http://www.mindworkshop.com/*).

GOTO KEYWORD ACCOUNTS

The search engine GoTo (*http://www.GoTo.com/*) came up with an interesting new strategy – your site will be ranked according to how much you pay for a keyword. Popular ones command higher prices and they are regularly auctioned. The costs can mount up, but so can the visitors.

REFERRAL FORMS

This is a good example of an automated marketing tool – something which helps you promote your web site 24 hours a day, 365 days a year and does all the work for you. An example is LetMeKnow (*http://www.letmeknow.com/*) which gives you a facility in your site whereby visitors can refer their friends. Unlike other referral services, LetMeKnow won't try to pinch your hits.

A CHECKLIST FOR E-BUSINESS

Do you have all you need? Have you done all you can?
    If you have a biggish site or business, do the following:

- register a domain
- get SSL from ISP
- get certificate from VeriSign (needs company documents)
- get merchant account or contact card clearing company
- design and upload your site to WSP/ISP
- get a shopping Cart program.

If you have a smaller site or business:

- register a domain
- join a shopfront system from a provider

- use site tools to produce your sub-site
- link to affiliate programs etc
- link to your main (home) site
- get orders by encrypted e-mail
- fulfil orders at home/work
- process card payments manually (with a biro) or pay extra to have provider do so.

A REGULAR 'GROW YOUR BUSINESS' PLAN

Daily

1 Answer your e-mail. People expect quick answers. Show them that you are on top of it.
2 Do one marketing task. It only takes 20 minutes to post an article to a bulletin board, register your site at a search engine or bulk e-mail a newsletter. So do one each day.
3 Search for your company name, keywords or related information and see where you stand in the ranking wars. If a new competitor pops up out of nowhere, you have a new challenge!

Weekly

1 Add more search terms to your goto.com account if you have one (see page 115).
2 Add new keywords to your web site meta tags. Check what tags your competitors use and incorporate them. Then unload your pages again.
3 Add something to your web site. Change a page by adding something to one of your pages. Or add a new page. The more points of entry your site has, the more visitors you will get. It also shows potential customers that your site is cherished and well-maintained.

Monthly

1 Find a new e-zine to advertise in.
2 Submit an article to e-zine publishers. Use the automated submission method described on pages 80 and 138.
3 Submit your web pages – including any new ones – to a new search engine.
4 Add your e-mail address and contact details to a new directory service.

Quarterly

1 Set up one new automated marketing tool. A referral form (see page 115), a new autoresponder or an additional e-mail handling tool can increase your traffic.
2 Establish a joint venture. Contact someone who sells a similar product or service to yours and ask them to offer yours as well. You will have to share your profits, but that's the price of increased sales. Equally, offer to promote someone else's product or service to your newsletter subscribers or web site customers, for a share of the income. But only do either of these with products, services and sites you can believe in. It's your reputation too.
3 Join a new Reseller or Affiliate program.

Annually

1 Revamp your existing e-business. Are the products tired? Is the service out of date? Could your entire web site do with a complete overhaul? Set aside some time each year to rethink it completely.
2 Start a whole new e-business. If one works well, two will work better. Do make sure it's something you know about or won't be embarrassed by. Just because a lot of people make money writing and selling software, don't try it if you can't write software. On the other hand, there are a lot of people who can write software but don't know about e-business. You do, however, so how about a joint venture?
3 Reward yourself. You've worked hard and you deserve to reap the rewards. So have a holiday, a good night out, a better car or something that says 'thank you' to yourself. You've earned it.

PART 2

Ideas for e-Businesses

KNOWING WHERE TO START AND KNOWING WHAT TO SELL

A good way to get ideas for what to sell is to check what does sell –
and then either do the same, or something completely different. (In
marketing-speak these options are known as 'following the wind' and
'sailing ahead of the wind'.) There are pros and cons to each, and you
can, of course, do both.

Following the wind – Pros	Following the wind – Cons
• If it's selling well already, there must be a market for it • You may be able to sell the same thing cheaper, have a wider range, deliver it quicker or find some other unique selling point (USP)	• If it's selling well already, somebody else has an established market – can you take it on? • Are you really going to set up in competition with a huge internet market organisation? Who would be brave enough to sell books against Amazon or WH Smith?
Sailing ahead of the wind – Pros • You may have a niche market nobody else is exploiting • If you create a new market you will have the first chance to exploit it.	**Sailing ahead of the wind – Cons** • If nobody's doing it already, is there a market for it? • You may have to create the market • If it's a good idea, rest assured someone with more muscle and a bigger promotional budget will start to consider the opportunity.

WHAT SELLS ON THE WEB I – SELLING 'NOTHING'

The easiest thing to sell on the web (and the one most often over-looked) is intellectual property – something that has no physical existence, or can be easily digitised for transmission. Three examples would be: professional services, documents and software.

Professional services

You may be an accountant and will use your web site to attract new customers, keep in contact with them and even receive and send financial information. The day cannot be far off when a paperless accounting system at a company can communicate with the accountant's computer and the bulk of the work done on a computer and by e-mail.

Equally, you may be a teleworker with a specialised skill – word processing, for instance, or spreadsheet, DTP or web design skills. I know of a number of disabled and able-bodied people who type up documents from hand-written faxes they receive at home, and others who do various types of document processing – brochure lay-out, for instance; or maintaining customer databases from hand-written response cards. The completed project is sent back to the client (or sometimes onto a third party such as a printer or a mailing house). Time sheets are sent in by e-mail and in some cases payments are sent electronically into a bank account on-line.

Documents

You may have some specialised knowledge which would make useful leaflets, information packs or 'how to' documents. Almost anything you know is saleable – gardening tips, DIY hints, tax facts, travel guides. If you don't have any ideas, or don't feel like turning them into documents, there are lots of companies which will sell you a CD-Rom packed with information sheets, and the right to sell these on all at once, singly or in groups.

Alternatively, you could market someone else's products. Online Originals (*http://www.onlineoriginals.co.uk/*) sells new fiction and non-fiction entirely on-line. These are new works, often by well-known and respected authors, but available only as downloadable documents. One of the books nearly won the Booker Prize, which says something about the quality of their list. Customers pay on-line and it's their phone bill for the download. The authors get 50% (usually £2) per book sold, which is more than they would receive from a standard print royalties agreement.

Journal and magazine publishers are turning to the web as a way of selling published articles, academic papers and subscriptions. Abstracts, expanded contents lists or abbreviated articles are available free to anyone, but you have to pay to acquire the full version. To get access to the latest edition of the magazine you have to register (so they can e-mail or post you other offers) or subscribe (pay an amount usually less than to receive the paper copy).

Good examples of this are the scientific press. Both *New Scientist* (*http://www.newscientist.com/ps/*) and *Nature* (*http://www.nature. com/*) operate full and very useful sites available to everyone, but the real gold and the latest stuff is available when you register and/or pay. And that's fine.

Likewise, academic publishers are turning more and more to provision of their journals on-line – you subscribe and have a password which allows downloading of papers of interest, or the whole issue. There is also access to a library of back-issues.

Academic book publishers have also spotted this one. They post the contents, chapter abstracts and selected chapters on the web, downloadable as Acrobat files (see Documents, page 126) but you need to pay to get a password which allows downloading of other chapters or the whole book.

Software

This may well be the largest sales sector on the web. Software houses and resellers list products with information about the programs, something which demonstrates it working and sometimes downloadable **freeware**, **shareware** or a **demo** for installing on your own PC to try out.

Freeware means just that – it's free after it's downloaded (or sent on discs) and you never need to pay. However, it may a version which has been disabled in some way (can't save, print or do some of the more interesting functions) or be an older version of a new program.

Shareware is distributed free on the understanding that if you like it, keep it and use it, you will pay. Sometimes it is disabled in the same way as freeware can be, and paying the buying price, licence or upgrade fee entitles you to the full or newer version.

Demos are usually less than full versions and often expire after a set time (30 days, usually) or a stated number of uses.

Software can be provided by download or on discs – increasingly, on CDs as programs get too big to fit on a small number of floppies.

As well as selling 'new' or their own software some companies bundle useful utilities, graphics, web page templates, databases and other useful programs and files onto CDs for selling. These tend to be the kind of programs which would be useful but which you would never really spend hours ferreting for on the web even if you knew they existed (such as the useful little add-ons typically found on PC magazine CDs), or large collections of clip-art and pictures for specific purposes (maps, photographs of famous buildings, engineering symbols, buttons for web pages), or lists (genealogical data, e-mail addresses, addresses of companies).

A lot of small businesses have sprung up based on the programming skills of one or a few people, selling small, cheap and useful applets (mini-programs running within another program) or add-ons (such as plug-ins). For instance, if I wrote an applet which ran in Microsoft Word and made your PC capable of putting the kettle on, getting the children bathed and pouring a glass of wine, and it cost £5, a bizillion people would probably buy it and I'd be rich. Sadly, I have no idea how to go about it, but I leave it to others as a concept.

Another rising trend is the provision of updates by download. You may not want to spend on-line time acquiring, say, a 200MB game, so you get the CD, but new inclusions, bug fixes, upgrade 'patches' (small segments of code which replace parts of the program installed on your PC), extra images etc are often free. In the case of, say, an anti-virus program, you might commit to an annual fee for unlimited upgrades and updates of new virus information as and when these are available.

The trick, as you will have gathered, is to provide the customers with something genuinely useful upon which they can make an informed (and positive) purchasing choice. Downloads which consist purely of screenshots of what a program looks like, or a version which is so non-functional that it doesn't provide any benefit, is unlikely to lead to a later, larger sale.

Catalogues

Imagine you sold screws, seeds, software or small arms. How about providing your customers with a downloadable catalogue which can be searched or browsed off-line whenever they wished? They could find products, select them for purchase and dial up to dispatch the order. It's cheaper, more convenient and quicker than an on-line search. For your part, you get to e-mail them the latest catalogue or updates, marketing and promotional information and news of offers, sales and deals.

PROVIDING DOCUMENTS AND FILES BY DOWNLOAD

The simplest way to provide textual and pictorial information on the web is just to have it on your site as web pages and let users browse it on-line. However:

- This may produce boring-looking text-filled documents.
- Pages filled with images may take ages to load.
- You may not want the information to be so readily available (eg you may want to sell it or restrict its availability to registered users). You could put such a document in a separate folder and password-protect it.
- Reading text on-line may be expensive in terms of phone charges and there may be too much to read.
- There is nothing to stop the reader saving the file for off-line reading later – you may want this, or you may not.

The alternative is to publish (on your web site) an abstract or extract of your document and to have the full version available as a download or to send it out on request. There are several ways to send out documents and other files.

As e-mail attachments

The customer provides an e-mail address as part of the ordering and payment routine and you reply with a 'thank you' e-mail to which the relevant file and any installation information is attached. The advantage to this is absolute control – you determine who gets what. The disadvantage is that you have to physically do it – you have to scan the incoming orders, produce a reply, attach the file and send it, using your phone line to do so. There are ways to minimise all of this:

- Have the reply e-mail and attachment available as a standard autoresponse setting (see page 55) which is sent after receipt of a valid ordering/paying e-mail.
- Wait until you have a number of orders and sent out the same (non-personalised) e-mail plus attachment to a number of customers. It lacks the individual touch and may put an unacceptable delay in the process – on-line customers usually want it *now*!
- You could set up a system where the customer gets e-mailed (instantly) with an autoresponse giving them the URL of a password-protected download site, and the password to go with it. This obviously involves setting up a download site (see below).
- Provide the file in a compressed format (zip, or a self-extracting executable, see below) which will reduce sending time.

If you can build in the costs of your phone bills and you feel the market will stand this, it is probably the simplest option.

A disadvantage is that you have to be sure the end-user has a MIME-compliant e-mail system. Since all e-mails, including attachments, are sent as text, data (in a program or a database, say) may get corrupted. This isn't a problem with the latest software, but there are still people out there using DOS-based text-only e-mail. This may not be their fault – it could be a company or college system they have no control over. But if you've taken their money, you have to provide the goods, which may involve you in additional expense posting out a CD or whatever. Put the appropriate warnings in your web page or literature.

As a download link in your web page
You will doubtless have seen these and may even have used them – a hyperlink says **Click here to download** which you do, and it does. This has its good points:

- It's not your phone bill (although you will have to upload the file to your ISP, which will involve your on-line time).
- You don't need to do anything – the user does it all.
- The file can be 'hidden' in a password-protected site or subsite if you don't want it to be free.
- If you do want it to be free, you can provide it (and as many more as you like) easily on your web pages.

But there are disadvantages too:

- The file may be too large to download conveniently. A 1MB file may take ten minutes or more, depending on the user's modem speed, the number of internet users at the time, the user's ISP's bandwidth, the physical distance between your server and the user (which means routing through more computers on its way) and other variables over which you have little control. This may not be an issue if the user doesn't pay his or her own phone bills – while at work or in a country with free local calls, for instance – but is a real disincentive for everyone else. Also, the longer the file takes to download, the greater the chance of the connection hanging, which may mean starting again. It may not be your fault, but you'll still get tainted by association.
- You can minimise some of this by uploading your files to 'local mirrors' – essentially, servers in different countries which contain copies of all your web site files. This costs extra, naturally, but may be worth it if it means you sell more. Ask your ISP if there is a deal with other providers elsewhere, or if they operate their own

mirror sites in Europe, the USA, Australia, the Far East etc.

- You have to get the file into a format suitable for downloading (see below).

Hints

1 It may be better, faster and more robust to have your download-able files available on an FTP site. Ask your ISP if there is an FTP server and upload your files to there. Make the links point to files in that server.

2 Ask your ISP if their server supports resumable downloads – there is nothing more frustrating than getting 95% of a one-hour down-load, then the phone cuts off. Or finding that the end has trun-cated. If resumable downloads are permissible, the user can dial in again and clicking the download link will pick up from where the last download left off. This turns an expensive, annoying cat-astrophe into no more than a minor irritation.

- Security is an issue. What is to prevent someone, anyone down-loading your entire web site, including the files tucked away in 'private' or protected folders? Basically, you have to either per-mit or disallow access to the various folders on your web site. You can provide 'everyone' with browse access (anyone who hits the site can see the files and by implication save them to their own PCs). You can also restrict designated folders to be password-pro-tected – put all such documents in a separate folder for this pur-pose. And for files you wish to sell, set them up on a separate FTP site from which downloading is just not possible without an access code. In all cases, ask your ISP or WSP how to achieve this. It may be possible for you to change the permissions manually for fold-ers – but you have to be confident that you know what you're doing. It may also be that the web design software you use lets you designate permissions for folders on your own hard disc, which are inherited by the server when you upload - FrontPage has this facility, although it isn't perfect.

FILES ON A DISC OR CD

If your files are huge or if there are lots of them, and if your market wants it, you should consider producing them on a CD. Even if you have downloadable files, you may want to offer the customers the option of getting a 'hard' copy as a CD. If you have lots of down-loads you could collect them together on a CD and sell this as a sep-arate product.

- To do this you will need your own CD **disc burner** (a laser CD recorder). These are available very cheap and if you are buying a new CD drive, consider a CD reader/writer to get the best of both worlds. You will also need **writeable discs** – be aware of the distinction between once-writable and rewriteable CDs and decide whether you want the end-user to be able to overwrite your material or not.
- You will also need CD labels and case inserts. The CD write program which comes with your CD burner may have label-generating software and you can buy sheets of CD labels to print on.
- This is fine for a small number of CDs or one-offs. Alternatively (and especially if you will be producing CDs in bulk) invest in a dedicated CD press or find a local company who can produce CDs to order from files you give them. If you can produce the original CD yourself (as above) it will be cheaper. The other advantage is that, unlike books which require large print runs to be economical, most CD pressing houses will consider small orders and produce them quickly. This means you are not paying large amounts up-front or keeping a large stock. On the other hand, you may want to do just that, in which case the price per CD will come down with volume.
- It is worth producing a larger number of labels and case inserts, especially if someone else is doing them for you. Take the trouble to have these well designed.
- CD houses may also take on the job of packing and posting out CDs for an additional charge. This may be worth while if your time is precious.

Much the same is true of files provided on a floppy disc. If your product will fit into 1.44MB, you can either copy to a pile of floppies using your own machine (a laborious process) or have someone do it for you, print disc labels and produce some sort of packaging. Consider whether you want the produced discs to be **write-enabled** (so they can be reused) or not.

DOWNLOAD AND DISC FORMATS

Whether you want to provide files and documents as e-mail attachments, downloadables or on disc or CD, you will have to consider their format.

Documents

It is best not to send document files as Word format (or any other text or word-processing format) unless you actively want the end-user to be able to edit and manipulate them. If you want the customer to be able to copy and paste from your document, or don't mind if they do, that's fine. Otherwise, package the file as Adobe Acrobat Portable Document Format (PDF). This is fast becoming the standard for document publishing and has a number of advantages.

- The files cannot be edited by the end-user – only viewed (and possibly printed out) using the Acrobat Reader.
- The Reader is free and is built-in to most modern browsers. You should, as a matter of courtesy, include a link to Adobe's download page from where anyone can download the Reader if they don't have it, or a newer version if they need it. This is at *http://www.adobe.com/* and the start page directs users to the nearest local mirror site to ensure faster downloading. At the time of writing the latest version was 3.0.
- Acrobat doesn't just handle straight text – highly designed DTP documents, image-laden catalogues, spreadsheets, data tables and even engineering drawings can be provided as Acrobat PDF files.
- The PDFs are highly compressed and therefore download faster than the equivalent Word or DTP source document.

The disadvantage is that although the Reader is free, the software to convert documents into PDFs isn't – you have to buy it from Adobe, or get a specialist agency to do it for you. Most design, print and graphics companies can do this, or the local college graphics department may be able to help.

Zip or self-extracting executables

If your file has lots of images, or if you have lots of files which you want to send together, these can be compressed and combined into a file format which will transfer quickly and easily over the internet. The best known format is **.zip**.

- Get a copy of WinZip (from *http://www.winzip.com/* or often found on PC magazine CDs). This fantastic program is one of the few pieces of try-before-you-buy software I have actually bought after the 21-day trial period because it is so useful. Apart from unzipping any files you might download, it allows you to zip up your own files either as the .zip format, or as a self-extracting executable file (a file with the extension .exe which, when clicked, expands into the source files without the user needing to have

WinZip or another program on the destination machine.

- The zipped files (or self-extracting executable) will be smaller than the source files, and combined into one single file which the user can expand back into the original forms.
- You can include folder information in the zipping process so that the path is recreated when unzipped – if you especially wanted the file to expand into c:/program files/goodstuff/newstuff/ you zip it from that location on your computer and it will unzip to the same (unless the end-user chooses otherwise).

Streaming and non-streaming media

- Audio, video and animation files can be provided in a variety of formats. The commonest for general multimedia are QuickTime, MPEG, MP3 and AV1. Most modern browsers can handle these as standard and once downloaded, can be played by the Windows Media Player or a specialised player (such as QuickTime). You will need the appropriate software to generate the files in the first place, or you may acquire them from somewhere else.
- MP3 is especially good for music and it is becoming increasingly common for music clips (or even whole tracks) to be available as MP3 downloads. If it's good enough for David Bowie . . .
- An alternative (or a way of providing a quick sample on your web site) is to have the files available in RealMedia (RM) or VivoActive formats. These **stream**, that is they play in real time without downloading after a brief 'buffering' delay. They do not download to the user's computer, so you are not giving anything away. The user downloads a small **metafile** (a text file with instruction about the source of your media file) and the player accesses the source directly from your server or elsewhere. However, you may choose to provide the media files as downloadables as well.
- The users will need RealPlayer or the Vivo plug-in to play the files – these may be built into the browser or they are available as downloads. RealPlayer G2 is the free version, itself download-able from *http://www.real.com/* but you may have to dig a bit to find the free download section. Also download RealProducer, which will let you assemble and package media files in Real for-mat.

WHAT SELLS ON THE WEB II – SELLING 'SOMETHING'

Not everyone can sell abstract or digitisable products. Until the day comes that we can teleport wine, chocolates, books and the like Star Trek style, there will always be a need to physically ship objects. That side of it is easy – the postal services, couriers and specialised parcel delivery companies will queue up to part you from your revenue for the privilege of handling your merchandise. On the other hand, a potential purchaser could probably walk a few streets and get the same product right away.

The web does not provide:

- immediacy of acquisition (for tangible objects)
- the essentials of the retail experience – touching, tasting, using the product (except software).

Therefore the web has to provide other benefits. Among these are:

- Comprehensiveness – no 'real' bookshop could ever stock all titles, but a web site could have details, images and extracts from (potentially) every book in print. Make sure your site contains nearly everything relevant.
- Anticipation of desire – buy a book from Amazon, fill in everything they ask you to, accept all cookies and they will contact you frequently with offers of similar books, new works by your favourite author and gifts because 'in two weeks it will be Alison's birthday and last year we sent her flowers on your behalf'. There are sites which will offer to send you e-mail reminders if you program in important dates – anniversaries, birthdays, dates when insurance policies fall due and so on. This is not altruistic on their part – they will be only to happy to offer you gifts, e-mail cards and better insurance deals at the same time. You can offer the same service – e-mails can be sent on specific dates to specific people.
- Hands-free – if I ever succumbed to buying a Methuselah of champagne I doubt I would carry it home just in case. Order it on the web and it gets delivered. Set up a good, reliable distribution system and have alternatives – extra charge for next day delivery, for example.
- Information – no wine merchant knows everything about every wine, but a web site could have expert tasting notes on anything you want. Likewise, no bookseller has read every book or even the reviews of every book; no record-shop sales girl has listened to every CD; no car dealer has driven every make and model; no

computer dealer could offer you a full price and feature comparisons. Make sure your site has as much information as possible on as wide a range of goods and services as possible.

- Accessory details – when was the last time you went into a shop and they didn't have what you wanted on display but suggested you went next door to look at it then come back to purchase it from them? Never? Shops are not in the business of referring you to other shops for information. But a web site can have links to other places – manufacturers' sites, reviews, technical documents – that are completely external. They are still there for you to use as a resource. Only make sure these 'foreign' pages open in a new window or a frame, so the customer doesn't get away from your site.
- Follow-on service – buy software and you will get access to the producer's technical support site; buy a car from certain manufacturers on the web and they'll give you access to a weather and traffic conditions site. Provide something extra and free as a 'thank you'.
- Reselling other people's products – this is such an important possibility that is worth taking on its own in some detail.

RESELLING AND AFFILIATE SCHEMES

You can sell books, CDs, software, documents, services and even whole computers without having to stock them or handle the orders. Amazon, CDNow and a host of other outfits will provide you with a link for your web site which takes users to the selling site, but with a 'tag' so the site knows they came from you. Then you will receive a commission for each customer you forwarded who bought something. Why is this to their advantage? You may be running a specialist web site (herbal products and gardening information, say) and your link could be to gardening manuals, herbals, aromatherapy books etc. A link from you – which could contain partial search information so only relevant books show up – is tantamount to a recommendation from a known expert and is much more likely to generate a sale than a cold browse. You can even direct them to individual books. Take a look at *http://www.fifeweb.net/books-byb.htm* for a particularly blatant example.

Affiliate programs will account for 10% of the £3.6 billion ($5.8 billion) of public consumer transactions on the web in the year 2000 and perhaps 25% of £20 billion ($35 billion) in total sales by 2002. Amazon's Associates Program has more than 320,000 affiliated web sites (and rising) at the time of writing.

There are several different types of affiliate programs

1 **Per click**: a payment for every visitor sent to the merchant's site through a banner or text link on your page, regardless of whether any sale happens. Rates are usually pennies per click, per visitor. You will see 'Please visit my sponsors' messages on sites, and these are usually per-click payment links.

2 **Per lead or bounty**: a one-time payment for each customer referred, usually £5–£15 ($8–$25) per customer, and often paid only if the visitor fills out a questionnaire or provides an e-mail address.

3 **Per sale**: a commission for each sale you generate, as with Amazon. The commission may be for that item only, for all purchases in a fixed period of time (month, quarter or year), or for all purchases made in one purchaser's lifetime. This last could take a while to collect, so watch out for it.

4 **Two-tier programmes**: a commission is paid on direct sales you generate, and on sales generated by other affiliates you recruit. Typical commissions are 10–15% for direct sales and 5% for others in your 'chain'.

The best affiliate program for your site is one which will generate revenue, regardless of the percentage stated. An engineering site isn't going to sell many Elvis Costello CDs, but it may sell a few technical books. A site dedicated to the memory of Slim Whitman won't make money out of an affiliate link to Health Products, but may sell books and music CDs on related subjects.

There are many affiliate schemes out there although most of them are American and not suitable – the overseas shipping cost of the product outweighs any cost saving, or the product or information is not applicable to a UK or European market.

Here are a few UK examples, on the strict understanding that this is in no way a recommendation for any of them, nor a testament to their quality or wealth-generating capability:

- Amazon.co.uk (*http://www.amazon.co.uk/* and *http://www.amazon.com/*) – have a link to both and use the facility to include an Amazon search engine 'preloaded' with subject material relevant to your site.
- CDNow (*http://www.cdnow.com/*) – likewise, promote CDs on line with your site subject. If your subject is aromatherapy, link to Mood Music. Link to the European version.
- Preloved (*http://www.preloved.co.uk/index.cfm*) – this is a second-

hand sales site with everything from holidays to houseboats. Become an affiliate and you effectively host a buy-anything service on your site, with a cut of each sale for you.

- UR Wired (*http://www.urwired.com/pages/links/html*) – this European internet games superstore stocks hundreds of PC, Playstation and Nintendo games. Everyone's buying them, so why not through your site?
- Shop And Save (*http://www.shopandsave.co.uk/*) – users browse through this extensive listing of well-known on-line shops and if they purchase, you get something for your trouble.
- Personal Connections (*http://www.pconnections.com*) – this company offers free web-based e-mail services. Anyone who signs up via your affiliate link will see your logo while at the Pconnections site. The idea is to develop visitor loyalty and to provide an easy way for them to get back to your site.

Appendix

Where to Get Tools and Resources

THE 'MUST SUBMIT' SEARCH ENGINES

Read Make Your Web Pages Search Engine Friendly on page 79, then submit to these sites. Each of them has an 'Add your URL' link somewhere on the start page. Remember to have a list of keywords handy.

AltaVista	*http://www.altavista.com*
Ask Jeeves	*http://www.askjeeves.com*
Direct Hit	*http://www.directhit.com*
Dmoz	*http://www.dmoz.org*
Excite	*http://www.excite.com*
Go	*http://www.go.com*
Google	*http://www.google.com*
Hotbot	*http://www.hotbot.com*
Iwon	*http://www.iwon.com*
Looksmart	*http://www.looksmart.com*
Lycos	*http://www.lycos.com*
Microsoft Network (MSN)	*http://www.msn.com*
Netscape	*http://www.netscape.com*
Northern Light	*http://www.northernlight.com*
Snap	*http://www.snap.com*
Webcrawler	*http://www.webcrawler.com*
Yahoo	*http://www.yahoo.com*

FREE ON-LINE PRESS RELEASE SERVICES

Comitatus	*http://www.comitatusgroup.com/pr/index.html*
M2 PressWire	*http://www.m2.com/M2 PressWIRE/index.html*
PRweb	*http://www.PRweb.com*
Webaware	*http://www.webaware.co.uk/netset/text/*

MESSAGE AND BULLETIN BOARDS

You can draw attention to your site by posting messages without too much overt advertising on message boards. These are some of the most-visited.

Forums List Universe	*http://forums.list-universe.com/*
Homebusiness	*http://homebusiness-websites.com/cgi-bin/index.cgi*
Talk Businessbug	*http://talk.businessbug.com/*
Ablake	*http://www.ablake.net/forum/*
E-zineseek	*http://www.ezineseek.com/forum/index.cgi*
Free Publicity	*http://www.free-publicity.com/cgi-bin/talk.cgi*
Her Computer	*http://www.hercomputer.com/board/index.cgi*
Profitalk	*http://www.profitalk.com/*
Profitinfo	*http://www.profitinfo.com/discuss/marketing/*
Profitlines	*http://www.profitlines.com/ipub/index/html*
The Illuminati	*http://www.the-illuminati.com/board/index.cgi*
Vicinities	*http://www.vicinities.com/successdoctor/*
Willie Crawford	*http://www.williecrawford.com/cgi-bin/index.cgi*
Wilsonweb	*http://www.wilsonweb.com/forum/*

LIST DIRECTORIES AND SEARCH ENGINES

CataList	*http://www.Isoft.com/lists/ listref.html*	The catalogue of LISTSERV lists. Over 17,000 lists included.
List of Lists	*http://catalog.com/vivian/in terest-group-search.html*	Maintained by Vivian Neou. Includes other related information.
Liszt	*http://www.liszt.com/*	Search a database of over 80,000 discussion groups.
Prodigy Mailing Lists	*http://www.goodstuff.prodi gy.com/Lists/*	Hosted by Prodigy but open to anyone.
Publicly Accessible Mailing Lists Reference.Com	*http://www.neosoft.com/ cgi-bin/paml_search/* *http://www.reference.com/*	Mailing list and news-group directory with over 150,000 discussion groups indexed.
TILE.NET/litserv	*http://www.tile.net/ tile/listserv/*	Search a database of Listserv-based discussion groups.

COLLECTIONS OF MAILING LISTS

AudetteMedia Discussion Lists	*http://www.audettemedia. com/*	Excellent topical moderated discussion groups offered here. List names include: I-Sales, I-Travel, I-Gourmet, l-Help, I-Shop, I-Animals, I-WinSoft, I-Invest, I-College, I-WebReview. You can't go wrong selecting from this group!
Bird Related Mailing Lists	*http://birding.miningco. com/msub5-mlists.htm*	
BulletMail	*http://www.bulletmail.com/*	Offers by e-mail on the topics you pick . . . 75+ topics! Bargains, free software, contests, business, music, travel, internet events, more!
A1A Computer Jobs Mailing Lists	*http://www.a1computer pros.net/*	Offers a variety of computer jobs and technical mailing lists.

EdWeb's K-12 Education List of Mailing List Discussion Groups E-Mail Topics	*http://edweb.gsn.org/* *http://www.emailtopics.com* */Internet/*	Subscribe to their free e-mail lists, broken down by business and other topics.
Gender-Related Electronic Forums	*http://www.umbc.edu/wmst* */forums.html*	Annotated, frequently-updated, award-winning listing of more than 400 women- and gender-related e-mail lists.
Humor Mailing Lists	*http://www.angelfire.com/* *pa/humorlists/index/html*	Over 300 listed. Maintained by Frank Rapp.
LAW LISTS INFO LAW-RELATED LISTSERVS	*http://www.lib.uchicago.edu* */~llou/lawlists/info.html* *http://www.regent.edu/lawli* *b/listsll-topic.html*	
listTool.com	*http://www.listtool.com/*	Collection of mailing lists with an easy subscriber interface.
Lsoft International's Lists	*http://www.lsoft.com/SCRI* *PTS/WL.EXE?XS=10000*	Lists with 10,000 or more subscribers.
Mailbase	*http://www.mailbase.ac.uk/*	Over 2,000 electronic discussion lists for the UK higher education community.
Mouse Tracks	*http://nsns.com/MouseTrac* *ks.tloml.html*	The list of marketing lists.
netvet – Veterinary & Animal Mailing Lists	*http://netvet.wustl.edu/vmla* *.htm*	

LIST USER RESOURCES

Cyber Teddy	*http://www.webcom.com. teddy/listserv.html*	Online guide to mailing list info and newsgroups.
Discussion Lists	*http://lawwww.cwru,edu/ cwrulaw/faculty/milles/ mailser.html*	Mailing list manager commands.
Impulse Research	*http://www.impulse-research.com/list/html*	E-mail discussion groups lists and resources forum.
Finding information through newsgroups and e-mail discussion lists	*http://www.tka.co.uk/ search/newsgrp.htm*	Part of The Search Centre, maintained by Traynor Kitching & Associates.
INFORMundi	*http://ourworld.com-puserve,com/homepages/ ajra/mailingl.htm*	Mailing lists on the internet. A generic PowerPoint presentation for a seminar on mailing lists.
IFLA's Internet Mailing Lists Guides and Resources	*http://www.ifla.org/l/ training/listserv/lists.htm*	
Inter-Links 'E-Mail Discussion Groups'	*http://alabanza.com/ kabacoff/Inter-Links/list-serv.html*	General info and links on using discussion groups.
Michigan State University	*http://ciber.bus.msu.edu/ busres/maillist.htm*	International business resources on the www: mailing lists.

HOSTING SERVICES AND LIST MANAGEMENT TOOLS

The Bolis Group	*http://www.bolis.com/*	
Coollist	*http://www.coollist.com/*	Free. Advertiser supported.
Cuenet Systems	*http://www.cuenet.com/*	
Maillists.com	*http://www.databack.com /maillists.htm*	Offers various mailing list services.
Dundee Internet Services	*http://www.dundee.net/isp /email.htm*	An authorised reseller of Lyris(TM) E-mail List Server software.
binMail	*http://www.binmail.com/b inmail*	Reasonably priced mailing list hosting service. Non-profit rates.
eGroups.com	*http://www.egroups.com/i ndex/html*	Offers free service for e-mail discussion groups. Advertiser supported.

E-Mail Publishing, Inc.	*http://www.emailpub. com/*	
Esosoft's Mailing List Service Expansion LLC	*http://www.esosoft.com/ mailinglist/ http://www.highwinds. com/HWSite/Expansion/ listmanagement/html*	Choice of advertiser supported free lists (50 subscribers or less) or commercial (paid) lists without restrictions – both multi-featured.
Internet Mailing List Providers	*http://www.cs.ubc.ca/ spider/edmonds/usenet/ ml-providers.txt*	
ListBot	*http://www.ListBot.com/*	The folks from Submit-It! offer this new free mailing list announce-ment service.
mail-list.com	*http://www.mail-list.com/*	
MAX e-Mailer & MAX e-Mailer Pro	*http://www.ismax.com/ test_drive.html"*	Web-based mailing list management service. Starts at $25 per month. Premium features available.
OakNet Publishing Free Listserver	*http://www.oaknetpub. com/*	Newsletter mailing accounts.
ONElist	*http://www.onelist.com/*	Advertiser supported, free mailing list hosting service.
POBOX.COM Mailing List Service	*http://www.pobox.com/ p3/other.html*	
Vivian Neou's 'Internet Mailing List Providers'	*http://www.catalog.com/ vivian/mailing-list-providers.html*	Nice synopsis of what's available.
Starfire Systems	*http://www.lists.kz/*	French mailing list provider.
SYSTONIC	*http://www.systonic.fr/ systolist/*	
Topica	*http://www.topica.com/*	New, multi-featured list management service. Check it out.
Web Site Post Office	*http://www.websitepost office.com/*	Free ad-supported mailing lists or opt for commercial no-ad version.

PROMOTION

In addition to the sites listed below, when promoting a mailing list be sure to go to the mailing list directories to submit your list.

Discussion and Mailing List Promotion	*http://jlunz.databack.com/ listpromo.htm*	A collection of resources to help promote your list. Sponsored by DataBack Systems.
EzineCenter	*http://ezinecenter.com/*	List your e-zine here.
FreeShop	*http://demo.freeshop.com/ corp/emailnewsletter. htm*	Build your subscriber base by partnering with FreeShop.
Guidelines for Publishing and Promoting an E-mail Newsletter	*http://www.trafficplan. com/newsltrtips.htm*	By Bob Elston.
The List Exchange	*http://www.listex.com/*	Trade mailing list sponsorships here. Includes other list promotion resources.
LISTSERV@ HYPATIA	*listserv@hypatia.cs.wisc. edu*	Mailing list to announce new mailing lists. Place Subscribe New-List in the message body to subscribe and find out more about posting information about your new mailing list. Reaches over 17,000 subscribers who want to know (and possibly pass on information) about your new list.

SOFTWARE TO HOST DISCUSSION GROUPS

Lyris Email Listserver	*http://www.lyris.com/*	
L-Soft ListServ	*http://www.lsoft.com/*	NT, 95, Unix, $600.
LWGATE	*http://www.netspace.org/ users/dwb/lwgate.html*	Mailing list WWW gateway. Install this Perl CGI script on your server if you run Listserv, Listprocessor 6, Majordomo or Smart List so that visitors to your web site can read about your mailing list(s), subscribe from there, read archives and more.
Revnet Groupmaster v 1.0	*http://www.groupmaster. com*	Web-based.
Shelby Group Lyris List Server	*http://www.lyris.com/*	NT, 95, $495.
StarNine Technologies ListStar	*http://www.starnine.com/ liststar/liststar.html*	Macintosh, $395.

LIST MANAGEMENT TIPS

Consider Types of Mailing Lists, and Consider Options for Mailing List Management	*mtotd44@turbocheck.com* and *mailto:mtotd47@ turbocheck.com*	Send a blank message and receive back, by e-mail, the information mentioned.
Effective Management of Discussion List and other E-Mail	*http://www.internetadver-tising.org/resources/email-management.html*	By Adam Boettiger, moderator of the popular l-Advertising discussion list.
The Emailian Newsletter	*http://www.emailpub.com/ Resource_Emailian.htm*	The newsletter for publishers who use e-mail as a publishing platform.
E-mail Publishing Resource Center	*http://www.emailpub.com/ Resource_Main.htm*	Articles on e-mail publishing to help you with your e-newsletters, company news, product announcements, etc.

E-Publisher Digest	*http://www.mmgco.com/ e-pub/*	Exclusive moderated discussion group for list owners, moderators and publishers of electronic newsletters.
List Owners Discussion Group	*ml-owners-on@mail-list.com*	To join, send a blank message. Hosted by Mail-list.com.
June 1997 Macworld Review	*http://www.macworld.com :80/pages/june.97/Reviews. 3713.html*	Mailing-list servers. LetterRip and ListStar Manage Mailing Lists With Ease.
Majordomo FAQ	*http://www.cis.ohio-state.edu/~barr/major-domo-faq.html*	Maintained by David Barr and The Ohio State University.
Majordomo List Owner's Guide	*http://www.-uclink. berkeley.edu/major/major. admin.htm*	Written by E. Elizabeth Bartley.
National Consultant Referrals	*http://www.referrals.com/ articles/*	This site includes articles on starting a mailing list.

E-ZINES

These sites will take e-zine articles and submit them for you.

Articles	*http://216.147.104.180/articles/submit.shtml*
e-zine articles	*http://www.ezinearticles.com/add_url.htm*
E-ZineZ Article Distribution Digest	*http://www.e-zines.com/publishers.htm*
Free Content e-zine	send a blank e-mail to: *Free-Content-subscribe@onelist.com*
Idea Marketers	*http://www.ideamarketers.com/*
MediaPeak	Subscribe by sending a blank e-mail to *e-wire-on@mail-list.com* Submit articles and a four-line tag to either *mediapeak@mindspring.com* or *submitnews@aol.com* Articles are at *http://www.mediapeak.com*
PublishInYours	Subscribe by sending a blank e-mail to *PublishInYours-subscribe@onelist.com* then post complete articles.

Web Source	*http://www.web-source.net/articlesub.htm*
Writer and Publisher Connection (companion e-zine to Web Source)	Send a blank e-mail to article *announce-subscribe@egroups.com*
WriteBusiness Articles Reprint	*http://www.writebusiness.com*
Writers & Publishers Online	Send a short summary to *submit@list-content.com*

Glossary

Note: some entries in bold in the book do not have a glossary entry, but are explained in the text. Consult the Index for these.

ActiveX. Microsoft's own programming components inserted into a web page to provide functions not available in HTML, such as video clips, on-line ordering and payments, or database access. ActiveX comes from two other Microsoft technologies called Component Object Modelling (COM) and OLE (Object Linking and Embedding). It applies to a whole set of COM-based technologies but is loosely used for ActiveX controls, a specific implementation of ActiveX. ActiveX controls can be implemented in a number of programming languages. This (like Java) allows considerable interactivity within web pages. It is specific to Internet Explorer (Windows 95/NT and later), but the Ncompass plug-in allows embedded ActiveX controls to work in Netscape.

Adobe Acrobat. Programs developed by Adobe Systems for creating and distributing documents electronically as Portable Document Format (PDF) files. These can be viewed with the Acrobat Reader. The Acrobat Reader, the best known Acrobat component, is freely available as a stand alone program or a *plug-in.*

AltaVista. The best web search tool.

anchor. An HTML tag that can act as a link to another location, or as a bookmark for a link.

AOL. America On Line – the world's largest on-line service provider.

Applet. A small, independent application (program) run from within another program, not directly from the operating system. The best known examples are *Java* applets. Soon, a word processor may not be a single, large program on an individual's PC but a conglomeration of applets (for text entry, spell checking etc) that will be called down from elsewhere exactly as needed. Nothing to do with Apple.

Archie. A database search tool for ftp sites, now superseded by web search engines.

attribute. One of three characteristics of a tag (element). Some are required and some optional. Some take values.

avatar. A graphic which represents a real person in a cyberspace system and which the user can direct to change depending on what they are doing (talking, walking etc). It is also another name, like root, for the superuser account on UNIX systems.

background. An overall colour for a web page which can be defined by a colour statement (BGCOLOR="RED") or an image file (BACKGROUND="imagel.gif").

bandwidth. Used loosely to mean the amount of traffic a server or carrying line can handle, and therefore its speed.

banner. Originally, an advertisement displayed on the results page of a *search engine*, generated in response to the searched term. Advertisers pay to have their ads displayed when keywords are searched by a browser ('keyword advertising'). Banners can also be inserted into web pages, using a Banner Ad Manager, which handles transitions of one ad to the next, usually timed. See also *Banner exchange.*

banner exchange. Web site designers or owners can agree to exchange *banner* ads with each other, thereby increasing the likelihood that their product or service will be seen by browsers. There are many Banner Exchange Programmes which will arrange this.

bookmark. Confusingly, there are two usages: One is a placeholder in a document – anyone familiar with word processing will have used these. The second is a feature which allows a web *browser* to save the address (URL) of a web page as a shortcut so it can be revisited. These are called Bookmarks in Netscape and *Favorites* in Internet Explorer.

browser. A web browser is an application which interprets the commands which make up HTML documents (web pages) and displays them as designed. The two most popular are Netscape Navigator/Communicator and Microsoft Internet Explorer. These are graphical browsers, which display images as well as text. Most modern browsers can present *multimedia*, though they may require *plug-ins.*

browsing. Finding and viewing web pages with a web *browser.* Searching the web for specific subjects.

bulletin board. An electronic message centre, usually for specific interests. Users *dial up*, read messages left by others and leave their replies or new messages. Bulletin board systems (BBSs) are good places to find cheap or free software. There are many tens of thousands of BBSs worldwide.

button. In graphical user interfaces like Windows, a small outlined area or graphic in a box that selects a command or option when clicked. Do not confuse with a mouse button.

CAD. Computer-aided design – a general name for programs which allow the manipulation of two- dimensional and three-dimensional graphics as an aid to design.

CD-ROM. Read Only Memory (ROM) on a CD-format disc. This is useful for storage and for delivering large amounts (up to 750 MB or more) of data in a convenient package. Data CDs are different from music CDs, but most modern computers can run both formats in the same drive.

CGI. See *Common Gateway Interface*.

CGI script. See *Common Gateway Interface*.

client. A computer connected to a server, often at a great distance.

clip art. Electronic illustrations provided in collections for insertion into a document or web page. Most clip-art packages provide illustrations in several file formats (bmp, *gif, jpeg*, wmf) so they can be used in various word-processing applications.

common gateway interface. A specification for transferring information between a web server and a CGI program designed to accept and return data, such as form processing. The browser sends data to a CGI 'script' (program) on the *server*, the script integrates the data with a database held on the server and the results are sent back as HTML to a web page. These CGI scripts can be written in many programming languages such as C++, Perl, Java, or Visual Basic, and many examples are freely available (see page 91). Other methods of achieving this are ISAPI (Internet Server Application Programming Interface, used by Microsoft) and NSAPI (Netscape Server Application Program-ming Interface).

Compuserve. The world's second-largest on-line service provider (after AOL).

cookie. A message sent to a *browser* by a web server. The browser stores the message in a file usually called cookie.txt and the message is sent back to the server each time the browser requests a page from that server. This allows the server to identify users and send them customised web pages, such as a welcome message with your name in it. The name stems from UNIX programming objects called 'magic cookies', tokens attached to a user or program which change according to the areas entered.

CPU. Central Processing Unit – the electronic 'heart' of a computer, which directs the other functions. Clock speed (eg 450 MHz) is a measure of how fast the CPU is and therefore how many processes it can carry out per second.

cyberspace. A term coined by William Gibson in his novel *Neuromancer* to describe a shared virtual reality environment, now more loosely used to mean the totality of what is on the internet.

dial-up. The mechanism which connects your computer via a modem to a Point of Presence (POP) and logs into your *Internet Service Provider* (ISP). The ISP provides information, such as the gateway address, and may need your computer's IP, address. See also *domain name*.

digital revolution. The use of computers to automate office and other activities – from word processing to accounts and including the growth of the internet, digital phones which use *e-mail* and the availability of video, music etc on-line and on computers.

directory. A folder which holds a series of related files on a computer. See also *directory list*.

directory list. A style of HTML formatting for web pages, usually presented as a bulleted list of items. Different browsers present these in different ways and some ignore the style completely.

DNS. Domain Name System – every internet site has a unique DNS (in the form 123.456.789.368) which is hard to remember, so *domain names* are used.

document. The HTML that constitutes a web page.

domain name. A name, such as mysite.co.uk, which identifies one or more IP addresses and takes the place of the actual IP address (such as 215.22.132.34). Every domain name has a suffix that indicates which top-level domain (.corn, .net, .ac etc) it belongs to. There are only a limited number of such domains. Domain names can be bought and registered.

dongle. There are two definitions. One refers to a small hardware device attached to a computer which controls access to a particular application, as a form of software licence protection. The dongle is usually attached to the PC's parallel printer port. However, it has also come to mean any software that provides a small but useful piece of functionality, such as a *CGI* script.

download. Copying data from a main source to a peripheral device, such as copying a file from an on-line service or a network file *server* to a local computer. It is also used to mean the process of loading a font into a laser printer's memory. The opposite of download is upload, which means to copy a file from your own computer to another computer.

drag and drop. Applications which allow the user to drag objects, using the mouse, to other locations on the screen, such as pulling a *link* from a web page to the PC's desktop. Modern operating systems like Windows allow drag and drop between applications – the user can create a picture with a graphics package and drag it into a word processor document or web page.

DTD. Document type definition. The specification of HTML.

Dynamic HTML. Dynamic HTML is a way of making the web page change according to the user's interaction. It goes beyond standard HTML to provide functions which make web pages richer and more interesting.

e-business. This is the overall term for conducting business on-line. It includes, but goes beyond, *e-commerce*.

e-commerce. Buying and selling products with digital cash, via Electronic Data Interchange (EDI) or using SSL technologies to handle credit card transactions.

electronic commerce. See *e-commerce*.

element. A component of the document type definition (*DTD*) which contains HTML markups, also called a tag and containing attributes, types and content.

e-mail. Electronic mail, the transmission of text messages over telecommunications networks. Every-one using the internet has an e-mail address, which always includes the @ symbol (eg j.smith@microsoft.com). Some e-mail systems are confined to a single network, say within a company or a university, but others have gateways to other systems, enabling users to send messages anywhere. Most e-mail systems include a text editor for composing messages, which can be sent to a recipient's e-mail address or to several users at once. This is called broadcasting. At its worst, it is spam.

e-zine. Electronic magazine, a web site designed like a printed magazine. Some e-zines are electronic versions of existing magazines, but others exist only in their digital format. Most e-zines are supported by advertisements but some charge a subscription.

FAQs. Frequently Asked Questions, a hypertext document, help file or web page with answers to common questions about some topic.

Favorites. The Internet Explorer version of *Bookmarks*.

filter. This can refer to a program which allows or prevents certain information reaching the browser – examples are Cybersitter or Net Nanny which prevent children accessing some areas of the web. Also, in graphics programs and image editors a filter is an effect applied to an image, like a lens filter alters the look of a photograph.

freeware. Copyrighted software given away free by the author, usually allowing others to use the software and pass it on, but not sell it.

Frequently Asked Questions. See *FAQs*.

FTP (or ftp). File Transfer Protocol – more than a protocol, more a mechanism for moving files between Internet sites. FTP log-in always requires a password but this is often the word 'anonymous', hence 'anonymous ftp sites'.

GIF. See *gif.*

gif. Graphics Interchange Format, one of two bit-mapped graphics formats (the other is *jpeg*) used in web pages. It supports colour and various resolutions and includes data compression, interlacing, transparency and other features which make it useful for computer-generated images. GIFs can be animated – essentially a series of GIFs which load one on top of another.

graphics. Refers to a device or program which enables a computer to display and manipulate images, such as a graphics card or graphics package (an image editing and creating program).

Graphics Interchange Format. See GIF.

hacking. Altering a program, usually in an unauthorised way and often to get around a password, by changing the programming code directly.

hits. The retrieval of a page or an image from a web *server*, often presented as visitor numbers in a Hit Counter. Hits often are a misleading indication of *traffic* since calling up a web page with a graphic would count as two hits.

home page. The main page of a web site, an index, table of contents, welcome page or password box.

host. A computer system (or its owner) which contains the data to be accessed by remote computer systems. Many companies host web servers – they provide the hardware, software and communications required by the server, but the content on the server can be provided and *uploaded* by others.

hot spot. See *image map.*

HotJava. A web browser from Sun Microsystems, authors of the *Java* language, not completely finished yet.

HTML. HyperText Markup Language, a specific example of *SGML*. The agreed standard for describing the contents and appearance of pages on the web.

HTTP hypertext. HyperText Transfer Protocol – an object-oriented protocol used by web servers. A mechanism for allowing text, graphics etc links to other locations, usually on a mouse click.

icon. A small picture that represents an *object* or a program.

image map. A graphic containing one or more areas (*hot spots*) of clickable links.

interface. Anything which allows connection. For instance, Windows is a graphical user interface (GUI) which allows a user to connect with the computer.

interlacing. A method for loading *GIFs* and *JPEGs* which handles them in stages, speeding download times.

internet. If you have to look it up, you shouldn't be reading this book.

Internet Explorer. Microsoft's web browser.

Internet Service Provider. A company or service which provides access to the internet and usually provides a username, password and *dial-up* phone number, plus the software to use these. ISPs (also called IAPs or Internet Access Providers) are connected to one another through Network Access Points (NAPs).

IP address. See *domain name*.

IRC. Internet Relay Chat – synchronous (ie 'real' time) text or voice communication over the internet, using computers, *modems* and phone lines.

ISP. See *Internet Service Provider*.

Java. A high-level, platform independent programming language developed by Sun Microsystems. Originally designed for handheld devices and set-top boxes it was modified in 1995 to take advantage of the need to create executable content within web pages. Java is an object-oriented language similar to C++, but simplified to remove features that cause common programming errors. Java interpreters known as Java Virtual Machines exist for most operating systems, so Java can run on most operating systems including UNIX, Macintosh and Windows. Small Java applications (*applets*) can be downloaded from a web server and run on your computer by a Java compatible browser, such as Netscape or Internet Explorer. Some pundits predict that the software sales industry is under threat, because soon all applications will be in the form of applets, downloaded as required.

JavaScript. Based on *Java*, this Netscape scripting language can integrate *HTML*, *plug-ins*, and Java *applets* to each other.

JPEG. Joint Photographic Experts Group and the graphics format it has defined (see *jpg*).

jpeg. A graphical file format, like *gif*, used to display high-resolution images on the web. It has user specified compression which can significantly reduce file sizes to about 5% of the original (an advantage when *downloading*), although detail is lost in the compression. It is especially good for photo-realistic colour images. Files have the extension jpg.

jpg. See *jpeg*.

link. In hypertext systems, such as the web, a link is a reference to another page or object which the user can visit when the link is clicked.

log on. To make a computer system or network recognise the user, usually by entering a username and/or password. Also called log in and login.

Lycos . One of the best web search engines which also carries adverts.

mailing lists. Lists of addresses, useful for e-mail marketing campaigns. A good source for these is *http://catalog.com/vivian/interest-group-search.html*, but see Appendix for others.

markup. Information for the browser which tells it how to display the HTML data. There are four different kinds: descriptive markup (*tags*), references, processing instructions and markup declarations.

meta tags. System meta variables, HTML tags which provide information about a web page or site but which do not affect how the page is displayed. Usually they hold information such as author, title, what the page is about, and keywords which indicate content. Many *search engines* use this information.

MIME. Multipurpose Internet Mail Extensions – the standard method for attaching non-text files to e-mail and sending them between computers, basically by turning them into (unreadable) text. A web browser will pair a MIME type with the right software for running it.

mirror site. A replica of another web site, used to reduce network *traffic* (*hits*) on a server or improve the availability of the site. This is useful when the original site generates too much traffic for a single server. Mirror sites can also increase the speed of access – a US-based web site mirrored in Sweden, say, will improve European users' access. Heavily used sites many have many mirrors in strategic locations worldwide.

modem. A device (MOdulator/DEModulator) which turns electronic data into sounds which can be passed along a telephone line.

Mosaic. The first, and now largely superseded, web browser. Thanks, *NCSA*. There are different versions of Mosaic, including Spry, owned by *Compuserve*. Mosaic may all but disappear when Compuserve changes to a version of Internet Explorer.

multimedia. The integrated presentation of text, graphics, sound, video and animation. Multimedia applications were uncommon until increases in performance and decreases in hardware prices made it possible for all PCs to display video and play decent sound. Because multimedia applications are large, they are usually stored and distributed on CD-ROM.

navigation. Finding the contents of a web site. Good sites have simple, obvious and intuitive navigation.

NCSA. National Center for Supercomputer Applications – the US academic institution where much of the good work on computers happens. NCSA invented *Mosaic.*

Net, The Net. The internet.

netrepreneurs. Entrepreneurs who have (or intend to) become rich by setting up or investing in internet companies and services.

Netscape. Netscape Communications, makers of Communicator, which includes Navigator, the most popular browser along with *Internet Explorer.*

newbie. A new user on an on-line service, particularly the web.

newsgroup. An on-line forum or discussion group. There are tens of thousands of newsgroups on the web, catering for every interest. To read and send newsgroup messages, you will need a news reader, a program which connects your PC to a news server.

object. Any item which can be individually manipulated, including images but also other kinds of software entities such as data and procedures to handle the data. A spreadsheet or a *button* could be an object within a web page, for example.

off-line. Not connected. A web page or e-mail message can be downloaded for off-line (ie local) reading later. See *on-line.*

on-line. Connected. Users are on-line when they are connected to a web service by a modem or network. Also used as one word (on-line).

PDF. Portable Document Format. See *Adobe Acrobat.*

PICS. See *RSAC.*

platform-indpendent. A program or other data which will operate on any computer, whether Mac, PC, UNIX or whatever.

plug-ins. Software which integrates *multimedia* (sound, video etc) and certain interactive capabilities into web browsers, especially *Netscape.* See *ActiveX.*

POP. Point Of Presence – a local computer where a user can dial in to get remote access to a server further away.

POP. Post Office Protocol – the way e-mail software gets mail from a server.

Portal. A web site or service offering a range of resources such as e-mail, newsgroups, *search engines*, links and on-line shopping opportunities. The first portals were on-line services such as Compuserve which provided access to the web via a specially designed *interface.* Now most search engines (AltaVista, Lycos etc) have become portals in an attempt to get and keep an audience who use them as their point of contact with the web.

RAM. Random Access Memory – computer memory used for running programs. The greater the amount of RAM the faster (in theory) applications will run. In practice, as programes become more and more complex, they take up more RAM to run. Therefore, computers are coming with more RAM installed. RAM can usually be extended if required.

RSAC. The Recreational Software Advisory Council, established to provide ratings for web and internet content. It uses the Platform for Internet Content Selection (PICS) infrastructure to provide ratings on sites.

rtf. Rich Text Format, a word processing standard developed by Microsoft for specifying formatting of text independent of the software package, making transfer of documents between packages (Word, Notepad, AmiPro) easier.

SCAM. The real definition is an acronym for SCSI Configuration Automatically, a subset of the PnP specification that provides plug-and-play support for SCSI devices. But to most of us it is the practice of appearing to offer something in a web site (free software, interesting pictures, the chance to make a million etc) that isn't really there.

search engine. A database and the associated programming which allows web sites to be searched and found using a *spider*. Almost 75% of *traffic* to most web sites comes from the 10 major search engines, including Infoseek, Lycos, Excite, WebCrawler, AltaVista, and Hotbot.

server. A computer which provides services on a network and actually holds the web sites. Also called a host.

SGML. Standard Generalized Markup Language – HTML is a specific example of this.

shareware. Software distributed free of charge, but with a small fee if you intend to use it. Usually registration provides support and updates. Shareware is cheap because it is usually offered directly to the customer by *downloading*, so there is little production, packaging or marketing cost. Shareware is not public-domain software or *freeware*.

spam. Electronic junk mail or newsgroup postings. Some people define it as any unsolicited e-mail, usually advertising sent to a mailing list or newsgroup. It is unpopular because it is unwanted and can clog up a server.

spider. A program that automatically fetches web pages to a *search engine*. When it finds a link in a web page it fetches the other page. Also called a webcrawler.

SSL. Secure Sockets Layer, a protocol developed by Netscape for sending documents securely over the internet. SSL uses a private key to encrypt data. Many web sites now use SSL to handle confidential user information like credit card numbers. Web pages that require SSL usually start with *https://* instead of *http://*.

surfing. Undirected web *browsing*, as opposed to searching for specific information.

tag. Descriptive markup around an element. There are two kinds,

<Start> and </End>.

Telnet. A method of establishing direct (and private) connections between two computers on the internet.

traffic. The activity on a communications system, or the number of *hits* to a web site or page.

Uniform resource locator. See *URL*.

Upload. See *download*.

URI. Universal Resource Identifier. See *URL*.

URL. Universal Resource Locator – a naming system for all resources available on the web – web pages, sites, server etc. The 'name' of a web site, such as *http://www.fifeweb.net/* A URL has up to six components, the first two being essential. Example: *http://info.uae.ac.uk:80/pages/homepage.htin#top*

- Protocol (*http://* or *ftp://*) – identifies the method used to access the data.
- Domain name (*info.uae.ac.uk*) – the server holding the information. Common suffixes are co or com (in the USA) – a company; ac or edu (USA) – a university; gov – a government body; mil – US military; net – a service provider; org – non-profit organisation (eg a charity). The domain name may also have a country identifier such as uk or fi (Finland).
- Port address (usually *:80*) – and usually omitted.
- Directory path (*/pages/*) – where on the server the files are located
- Object (*homepage.htm*)- the actual web page or other resource.
- Spot (*#top*) – a specific place in the web page, requiring an anchor.

USENET. A worldwide *bulletin board* system that can be accessed through the web or other on-line service. USENET has more than 15,000 forums called newsgroups and is accessed by millions of people daily all over the world.

Version 4 browser. Any version of Netscape Navigator or Netscape Communicator above Version 4.0 and any version of Internet Explorer above Version 4. By a coincidence, Netscape brought out Netscape Communicator 4.0 around the same time as Internet Explorer 4.0, both of which had added functionality, such as the ability to run *Java, Dynamic HTML* and *ActiveX*.

virus. A program or piece of code loaded onto a computer without the user's knowledge, often carried with another program. Most viruses can replicate – make a copy over and over again – which will soon use all available memory and hang the system. Some viruses can transmit themselves across networks and overcome security systems. A worm is a type of virus which can replicate itself and use up memory, but does not attach itself to other programs.

VRML. Virtual Reality Modelling Language, a specification for displaying three-dimensional objects on the web. VRML files have a .wrl (short for 'world') extension. To view these files, you need a VRML browser or a VRML plug-in to a web browser.

web browser. See *browser*.

web cam. Or webcam – a video camera which sends images to a web page.

web ring. Virtual communities of web sites with linked *navigation*, usually free of charge to visitors and members but carrying paid advertising.

webmaster or webmeister. A job title that didn't exist a few short years ago – a constructor, organiser and foont of all wisdom on web pages. Once a lonely, sad individual working away at midnight in a deserted computer room, the webmeister is now a highly regarded and well-paid position in many large companies.

Winsock. Short for Windows Socket, an Application Programming Interface (API) for developing Windows programs that can communicate with other machines using the TCP/IP protocol. Windows 95 and /NT come with Dynamic Link Library (DLL) called winsockAll.

wizard. A helper utility in an application that leads the user through the steps of a process, such as installing software.

WWW (The Web or W3). The World Wide Web, one component of the internet and the most popular.

zip file. File compressed with the ZIP format, which unzips to one or more files. This is not to be confused with the zip drive, a high-capacity drive developed by Iomega Corporation. Zip discs are slightly larger and thicker than floppy discs but can hold 100 MB of data, useful for backing up hard discs and for transporting large files.

More computer and internet definitions are available on-line at: *http://webopedia.internet.com/*:

Further Reading

Using the Internet, Graham Jones (How To Books, 1999).
Creating a Web Site, Bruce Durie (How To Books, 2000).
Doing Business on the Internet, Graham Jones (How To Books, 1997).
1000 Best Web Sites, Bruce Durie (How To Books, 2000).

Index